Stiven Tremaria
United Nations Peace Operations Revisited

I0096257

WIFIS-aktuell
Book Series

Edited by

WIFIS – Academic Forum for International
Security, represented by

Prof. Dr. Johannes Varwick, Martin Luther
University Halle-Wittenberg

Volume 78

Stiven Tremaria

United Nations Peace Operations Revisited
The Case of Haiti

Verlag Barbara Budrich
Opladen • Berlin • Toronto 2026

A CIP catalogue record for this book is available from
Die Deutsche Nationalbibliothek (The German National Library):
https://portal.dnb.de.

© 2026   by Verlag Barbara Budrich GmbH, Opladen, Berlin & Toronto

    ISBN   978-3-8474-3074-2 (Paperback)
    eISBN 978-3-8474-3364-4 (PDF)
    DOI   10.3224/84743074

Verlag Barbara Budrich GmbH
Stauffenbergstr. 7. D-51379 Leverkusen Opladen, Germany | info@budrich.de |
www.budrich.de

86 Delma Drive. Toronto, ON M8W 4P6 Canada | info@budrich.de | www.budrich.eu

Cover design by Walburga Fichtner, Cologne, Germany
Typesetting by Angelika Schulz, Zülpich, Germany

Table of Contents

Figure: Political Map of Haiti
Source: International Crisis Group (2025: 29)

1 Introduction

On 30 September 2025, the UN Security Council (UNSC) approved by Resolution 2793 the launch of the thirteenth peace operation in Haiti: the Gang Suppression Force (GSF), which as the name indicates, is mainly aimed at conducting – in cooperation with the Haitian police and armed forces – targeted operations using coercive force to neutralize, isolate and deter the criminal gangs that currently de facto control over 85% of the capital Port-au-Prince and the departments in the country's center, terrorize the civilian population through serious human rights abuses, are linked to transnational organized crime, and threaten the very existence of the Haitian state and its monopoly on legitimate violence (UNODC 2025). Thus, the GSF is the response by the UN to deal with the ongoing crisis in Haiti, which is not about a conventional war but an irregular and asymmetric conflict between weak and dysfunctional state security forces against logistically well-organized and better-equipped criminal gangs.

UN engagement in Haiti in the form of multinational peace operations began more than three decades ago and, so far, it shows a poor track record in managing and solving Haiti's deep political, economic and social crisis, as the country has repeatedly relapsed into cycles of instability and violence, to the point that it is currently on the brink of state collapse since 2021. The launch of the GSF is an auspicious occasion for critically revisiting the debate on "the futility of force" (Cockayne 2014) by UN peace operations in dealing with unconventional armed non-state actors for broader stabilization purposes through an in-depth examination of the case of Haiti. Therefore, the research subject of this study only encompasses those missions deployed by the Security Council under Chapter VII of the UN Charta that are authorized to use force to help local security forces to counter identified peace and security threats, and restore and secure state political authority and territorial integrity. Currently, the UN has just 11 peacekeeping missions on the ground, of which only three are of them are of this type: the UN Stabilization Mission in the Democratic Republic of the Congo (since 2010), the UN Mission in South Sudan (since 2011) and the UN Multidimensional Integrated Stabilization Mission in the Central African Republic (since 2014) – and most lately, the newly launched (but not yet fully deployed and operational) GSF in Haiti. Although the debates on the use and futility of coercive force from the international relations and peace and conflict research are not new but have been central and recurrent in broader discussions about the purposes, practices and identity of UN peacekeeping since around three decades, this newest launched mission provides an occasion to rekindle this critical discussion, so this booklet aims at summarily revisiting this debate and its critical issues by performing an up-to-date analysis of a very topical case, such as Haiti.

Haiti is an extreme but highly illustrative case for reexamining these paradoxes. Haiti is an island state located in the Caribbean Sea, with a land area of 27,750 km2 (similar in size to the German federal state of Brandenburg) and an estimated population of 11.9 million, of whom nearly 3 million people live in the metropolitan area of Port-au-Prince. With 59% of the population living below the poverty line – of which 38% are in extreme poverty (on less than USD 1.25 per day) – and a life expectancy of about 61 years, Haiti has been regarded for decades as the poorest country in the Americas, one of the nations in the lowest 15% globally on the Human Development Index and one of the world's top-10 failed states, due to the government's inability to perform basic functions such as delivering public services, ensuring domestic order and monopolizing legitimate violence, meager political governance, generalized mismanagement and endemic corruption, absence of the rule of law and low socio-economic development (The World Bank 2025, Fragile States Index 2024, UNDP 2023). Haiti has been selected as a case study not only because of the acute state collapse caused by gang activities – which has been making headlines in the international media in recent years, but also since the country is highly illustrative of the paradoxes surrounding the futility and effectiveness of the use of force by peace operations, especially when considering that the country has hosted the largest number of missions throughout the entire history of UN peacekeeping (see section 4). Haiti is therefore an extreme case of a long-standing and chronic failed state with a structural inability to fulfill its basic functions and monopolizing coercive violence, and where consecutive and resource-intensive international interventions have been incapable through various means of completely breaking down the criminal gangs and rendering the state both stable and functional.

This study bears academic and practical relevance for critically reviewing the rationale and performance of UN peace operations concerning the use of coercive force in Haiti. On the one hand, a temporary gap of nearly a decade exists in the academic discussion on the performance of UN missions in Haiti: While the UN Stabilization Mission in Haiti (MINUSTAH) received considerable attention among the circles of scholars and practitioners in the 2010s, the most recent developments over the 2020s, including the launching of the Multinational Security Support Mission in Haiti (MSS), have been very poorly addressed through theory-driven scholarly contributions. On the other hand, a critical assessment of the strengths and shortcomings of the two above-mentioned peace operations in using force to counter Haitian gangs and foster state stabilization will serve, from a practical standpoint, to outline a series of policy recommendations for the newly launched GSF and future engagement by the international community in Haiti. The analysis provided in this study is underpinned by a critical examination and documentary analysis of primary and secondary sources. Primary sources include UN resolutions and reports, while secondary sources comprise books, journal articles, working papers, reports from non-government organizations and think tanks, and carefully selected news articles.

The remainder of this booklet is structured in four sections. Section two provides a theoretical review on the genesis of use of force practices by stabilization missions and outlines five critical elements surrounding them: the ambiguity of their mandates, the tension with the principle of impartiality by peace operations, the disposal of required operative and tactical capabilities, the negative unintended consequences of using force, and its ultimate purpose as a means to building political and societal peace. In the third section, the framework under which these missions operate in the selected case study is contextualized, offering a brief socio-political overview of Haiti and a characterization of the genesis and evolution process of Haitian criminal gangs. The fourth section examines in detail the performance of the two missions (MINUSTAH and the MSS) previously authorized by the UNSC under Chapter VII powers to deploy coercive force for stabilization purposes in order to counter the gangs and uphold the authority of the Haitian state, based on the five critical elements outlined above. Finally, a comprehensive assessment of these experiences is provided, for later drawing up a batch of recommendations for the future work of the GSF and fostering the sustainability of the state, overall reconstruction and societal peace in Haiti.

2 The Use of Force by UN Peace Operations

Despite its widespread reference in international treaties, resolutions of inter-state organizations and political discourse, the use of force as a performance principle by UN peace operations lacks a precise and clear definition of its nature, rationale and boundaries of practical application under international law. In military and police contexts, use of force denotes the amount of physical power or coercion deployed usually to make someone comply with certain rules and norms, or stop an immediate threat – unlike in cases of aggression aimed to defeat and annihilate an enemy (Friesendorf 2012: 10–18). Thence, the use of force by peace missions may encompass two modalities: the deployment of coercive strength for preemptive and reactive measures, or taking anticipatory and offensive action against perceived peace-breakers (Williams/Bellamy 2021: 310). In practice, the use of force ranges from one end of the spectrum to low-intensity physical restraint up to the opposite end, entailing the application of large-scale lethal force through the employment of firearms and destructive weapons. In most domestic and international legal standards, the resort to force is generally regarded as justified and appropriate when the following six criteria are met: necessity (the lack of safer viable alternatives), proportionality (the positive correlation between the level of force employed and seriousness of the threat or offense), lawfulness (the pursuit of a legitimate objective), distinction of the object/ target (transgressor versus others, or combatants and civilians, respectively), the observance of proper rules of engagement (namely, those established procedures and operative regulations to be followed when force is deployed) and accountability (liability in the event of misconduct) (Ekanayake 2021: 144–148, 161–162, 197–198).

The use of force by peace operations mirrors a doctrinal and practical evolution in the development trajectory of UN peacekeeping missions since the Cold War until today. Based on the taxonomy posed by Kenkel (2013: 123–125), the historical progression of peace operations' practices may be traced in "generations", as a theoretical and analytical construct to give contours on the changes and adaptations experienced by such missions over time concerning the type of tasks conducted, the level of physical force authorized to be employed, and the actors engaged in such endeavors. Peace operations launched by the UNSC emerged originally based on the so-called "Holy Trinity of Peacekeeping", underpinned by three traditional principles:

host-state consent, impartiality relative to the conflicting parties and non-use of force – except in case of self-defense. Under these principles, a "first generation" of peace operations was launched throughout the Cold War under the umbrella of the Chapter VI of the UN Charta on Pacific Settlement of Disputes for monitoring and ensuring the observance by conflicting parties of temporary truces, ceasefires or formal peace agreements through the deployment of an interpositional buffer force – mainly watched by lightly armed blue helmets – between the frontlines for monitoring borders and verifying demilitarized zones (Kenkel 2013: 125–126). These tasks were followed by a "second generation" of peace operations in the early post-Cold War era between the start and mid-1990s after the release of the *Agenda for Peace* (1992) by former UN Secretary General Boutros-Ghali, "characterized by the addition of civilian tasks related to political transition from conflict, without an accompanying increase in permission to use military force" (ibid.: 128). Among the new activities added to traditional first-generation military mandates stand out humanitarian aid delivery, refugee assistance, organization of elections, support to disarmament, demobilization, and reintegration programs for former combatants, and government capacity-building programs.

The cruelty experiences of genocidal violence during the wars in Rwanda (1994) and Bosnia and Herzegovina (1995) – which occurred largely in front of the helpless eyes, paralysis and inaction by UN peacekeeping missions on-site – led to a critical rethinking of the scope of the use of force by peace operations when serious human rights violations and crimes against humanity occur in the context of civil or international conflicts. This gave rise to a "third generation" of peace operations during the late 1990s and early 2000s under the umbrella of Chapter VII of the UN Charter on Actions with Respect to Threats and Breaches of the Peace and following the recommenddations of the *Brahimi Report* (2000), which clearly called the UNSC – either through blue helmets or regional organizations and coalitions of states – to use high-intensity physical force for mandate enforcement purposes, even without the host state's consent (ibid.: 130–131). Doctrinally and legally, the mandate for these operations – labelled under the negatively politically-laden concept of "humanitarian interventions" – was justified under the emerging principles on the responsibility to protect civilians in the face of the commission of atrocity crimes (genocide, war crimes, crimes against humanity and ethnic cleansing) and the protection of civilians during armed conflicts in line with principles of international humanitarian law, as stated in the Geneva Conventions (cf. Foley 2017, Thakur 2018, Hunt 2019). Even in some of the few cases where peace missions were launched under these premises (i.e., Kosovo or East Timor), the UN later established mixed interim administrations for post-conflict peace and statebuilding, where certain areas (such as civil administration, police and justice, defense, reconstruction and economic development) were placed under the steering of local and/or international actors – thus giving rise to a "fourth generation" of peace operations (Kenkel 2013: 133).

Since the early 2010s, the doctrine on the use of force has evolved to deal with more hostile and complex conflict environments, encompassing state-building and stabilization goals through the fight against armed non-state actors of a terrorist nature, extending and consolidating state political authority, and preserving territorial integrity. Hence, the use of force has become legitimated in practice not only for defensive and deterrence purposes to curb spoilers threatening peace – as originally delineated in the well-known *Capstone Doctrine* (2008) – but also to enforce the mission's mandate geared toward fostering stabilization and counterterrorism – in the sense of physical containment of aggressors and spoilers to maintain order and ensure state integrity – in scenarios where there is no peace to keep by neutralizing and defeating a designated enemy (cf. De Coning 2018, Karlsrud 2018, 2019; Williams/Bellamy 2021). These goals have been pursued by using a combination of integrated military and police actions to tackle violence and state collapse by coercive means – so giving rise to a "fifth generation" of robust peace operations by multidimensional integrated stabilization missions, as deployed in a few cases worldwide, like the Democratic Republic of the Congo, Mali, South Sudan, Central African Republic, Somalia and Haiti.

The practical implementation of the doctrine on the use of force for stabilization and statebuilding aims by UN peace operations has spawned rich, extensive and critical debates in the contemporary literature on international relations and security policy by renowned scholars and practitioners worldwide (cf. Nadin 2018, Hunt 2017, 2019; Foley 2017, Thakur 2018, Karlsrud 2018, 2019; Berdal 2019, Ekanayake 2021, among others) – whose thorough review considerably exceeds the scope and length of this brief study. In order to deliver a brief critical review about the rationale and performance of UN peace operations in the Haitian case, which accounts for the achievements and drawbacks commonly observed by those missions tasked to use large-scale coercive force for dealing with armed non-state actors, this paper focuses solely on five key issues, grounded on existing theorization from the specialized scholarly literature. To this end, this section roughly outlines the central arguments – for and against – posed by scholars for each critical issue, thereby providing an analytical framework to address the empirical case study in section 4 of this paper.

First, mandates for the use of force in stabilization missions are characterized by a certain degree of ambiguity and lack of clarity. From a doctrinal standpoint, "there is no internal document within the UN that attempts to explain what the stabilization concept means in the context of UN peace-keeping doctrine, nor does there seem to be any appetite for undertaking such a conceptual or doctrinal review process" (De Coning 2018: 87). As stabilization missions are commissioned and deployed in scenarios of ongoing conflicts where there is no peace to keep due to any agreement among the conflicting parties or military defeat, they are usually authorized in loose and vague terms to use force to achieve a stable environment by all measures possible – but both means and end often remain ambiguous due to unclear mandate and boundaries. At the operational level, ambiguity in the mandates for the use of force has resulted in different understandings "among troop-contributing countries about how mandates should be interpreted and, specifically, over attitudes to the use of force, [… which] has further undermined efforts to achieve force cohesion and unity of purpose" (Berdal 2019: 122). Based on a detailed review of UNSC resolutions entailing use of force's mandates, De Coning (2018: 90) outlines a narrow definition of stabilization missions:

1. they are mandated to contribute to restoring and maintaining stability by
   a. helping to protect the government and its people against identified aggressors;
   b. helping the government to reclaim control over territories previously controlled by such aggressors;
   c. helping the government to extend the authority of the state throughout its territory;
2. they operate in support of and alongside the security forces of the host nation, and their mandates often include supporting efforts to build the capacity of these national forces; and
3. they are mandated to use force robustly in the face of anticipated attacks against themselves and those they are tasked to protect, and encouraged to do so proactively.

From this definition, it follows that UN stabilization missions are essentially underpinned by a security and military-centric understanding of conflict management (Karlsrud 2018: 89) by being legally authorized – in support to or replacement of local government's security forces – to use high-intensity physical force against armed non-state groups – categorized as "peace aggressors" and "illegitimate parties of the conflict" (De Coning 2018: 91), neutralize them and degrade their capacity for action, extend and secure state (political) authority, and protect civilians by all necessary means possible (Karlsrud 2019: 87). The latter means involve the performance of both defensive and offensive targeted – or even undifferentiated – actions against identified enemies under a war-fighting paradigm (Williams/Bellamy 2021: 316–317).

Second, the identification of aggressors and the deployment of coercive force against them bring fundamental tensions with the core principle of impartiality by peace operations, as by engaging in large-scale reactive and proactive combat actions against one of the factual conflict actors, peacekeepers risk to erode their impartial character and become de facto warrying parties on behalf of the counterparty, as the use of force is usually authorized and deployed – either unilaterally or jointly – in support of the country's government (Ekanayake 2021: 91). Under this sort of missions, the dividing line among peacekeeping, peace enforcement and war making blurs, as the intended purpose of UN peace operations for neutral conflict management takes on the contours of war by adopting a position toward a targeted enemy, whose aim is imposing one's will on it by neutralization and defeat – and such a labelling "provides moral justification for targeting such types of combatants with elevated levels of force along the lines used on an adversary in war" (ibid.: 92).

Consequently, the use of force by stabilization operations comes to challenge traditional principles of peacekeeping, as their positioning regarding the conflicting parties clearly unbalances in favor of the current state's government, as "these types of missions create a structural relationship between the host government and the UN that leaves little room for engagement with non-state actors and civil society, especially at the local level, and that limiting the role of the UN mission to engaging principally with the host government weakens the likelihood of the mission contributing to sustaining peace" (De Coning 2018: 93). Hence, the way in which a peace operation acts and its perceived impartiality in relation to major disputants may have far-reaching implications for shifting the conflict dynamics and for the credibility and leverage of UN missions in general (Berdal 2019: 124). For stabilization missions, legitimate concerns have been raised whether impartial peacekeepers, by standing on the government side, just help to enforce illegitimate and "unilateral political solutions through support of a government's statebuilding ambitions and its attempts to extend state authority [...] by pursuing military victories through the offensive use of force" (Williams/ Bellamy 2021: 314–315). This may be particularly critical in settings where the grievances and aspirations upheld by armed non-state actors enjoy greater legitimacy and support among the general population than central governments seated at the capital, or state security forces are the major source of insecurity, violence and human rights violations against civilians. Notwithstanding this valid criticism, "theoretically, in some cases it may be possible to align impartiality with limited offensive measures against violent groups, if these are seen as externally driven and motivated, and not representing the local population" (Karlsrud 2018: 100).

Third, in order to achieve their aims, stabilization missions with use of force's mandates require having at their disposal the operational and tactical capabilities necessary to undertake these kinds of operations effectively and by inflicting the least possible damage. By appropriate capacity is meant "how the force is organized and deployed, the kind of command and control model applied, the type of equipment needed, and the way the peacekeepers are trained and prepared" (De Coning 2018: 95). Critical voices have skeptically contended that effective use of force by peace operations is usually operationally inviable since "peacekeepers are undermined by UN's perennial constraints, such as weak political support, the erratic availability and quality of troops and equipment, and the reticence of troop contributors to embrace a robust approach" (Williams/Bellamy 2021: 319). And when operations have tried to realize their strategic objectives "in a political vacuum without proper resources, the medium to long-term consequence of their actions have been, more often than not, to destabilize the operating environment and complicate the search for political solutions" (Berdal 2019: 127). The reasons for this poor record lie not only in those practical challenges that inherently missions face as a third party in highly complex scenarios of open conflicts, but largely in "the intergovernmental and intensely political nature of the organization, which will always limit the degree to which a UN force can work as a truly integrated, cohesive and effective military force" (ibid.: 120).

Therefore, to be successful in fulfilling their mandate, high-intensity force operations should entail well-equipped, properly trained, competently led and highly capable forces combined with strengthened command and control, the availability of modern technology, logistics and engineering, aviation and maritime strength; financial support, onsite-based tactical intelligence and ideally local support (Karlsrud 2018: 97, Berdal 2019: 119). Of these requirements, arguably one of the most compelling relates to "the need for more systematic local-based intelligence collection, assessment and conflict analysis capacities by UN missions, the lack of which in zones of conflict has critically undermined attempts to grapple with underlying political economies of conflict and the way in which these often drive violence and encourage predation against civilian populations" (ibid.: 122).

Fourth, proper and effective use of force may generate a series of negative repercussions, collateral damages and short- and medium-term risks that can jeopardize the very existence, viability and long-term effectiveness of peace operations. These unintended consequences encompass all those effects, outcomes and impacts that are not intended per se in the mandate of such missions and fall outside the scope of the response expected to achieve (cf. Aoi/De Coning/Thakur 2010). As claimed by Hunt (2017), the "robust turn" of peace operations at an operational and tactical level may trigger a series of negative unintended consequences that undermine the very sense and character of these missions as tools for conflict management and resolution across six different dimensions: vulnerable civilians, safety and security of UN personnel, humanitarian access, local human rights situation, post-conflict peacebuilding and development, and the political settlement of the conflict. Above all, the application of coercive force may cause an uncontrolled escalation of violence, redounding in a higher vulnerability, attacks, injuries and fatalities by peacekeepers, civilian personnel and their facilities, but also collateral damage on civil population caught in the crossfire or mistaken for difficult-to-identify enemy targets, or due to revenge attacks on civilians deemed cooperating with the UN (Hunt 2017: 115–116). Although unintended consequences by the use of force are to a large extent fully unavoidable, as this type of operations inherently entails a high degree of physical violence and takes place in challenging, disrupted and unforeseeable environments (cf. Aoi/De Coning/Thakur 2010), what is important for minimizing their potential negative effects are clear and observed rules of engagement governing the performance of these operations (Ekanayake 2021: 200–201) and putting in place multilayered, internal and external reporting, accountability and prosecutorial mechanisms in case of malpractices or human rights violations during high-intensity force operations, as well as – where necessary – providing adequate financial compensation for civilian victims and their families (Di Razza 2020: 4–5, Karlsrud 2018: 101).

Moreover, the use of force may sometimes significantly undermine the possibility to achieve a political agreement among conflict parties, as "the employment of coercive means to enforce a particular form of peace militates against the most inclusive types of politics [… and may] have ramifications for the sustainability of the peace" by forcibly silencing the voices and demands held by those stakeholders labelled as aggressors, thus "perpetuating and reproducing the precise root causes of conflict that missions are sent to address" (Hunt 2017: 124–125). In line with this, some critics have rightfully claimed that the use of force may reduce the space for political dialogue, prolong the intensity of conflict and make conflict resolution and peacebuilding more cumbersome (Williams/Bellamy 2021: 318).

Lastly, and in conjunction with the last point above, the use of force by stabilization missions must not be conceived as an end in itself, but rather as a means framed within a broader political strategy aimed at conflict resolution. Hence, deploying high-intensity coercive force should not be misunderstood as a mere attempt to ultimately solve conflicts by military means, instead as a component part of a larger strategy aimed to conflict management through proactively shaping the security environment by containing aggressors in order to lay the groundwork for comprehensive solutions to political and social problems (De Coning 2018: 90). In this sense, at a tactical level, it does make sense to just deploy a properly equipped and composed mission to employ decisive and targeted high-intensity force to deal with serious crises and threats, but at a strategical level, robust peacekeeping should ideally be closely aligned to and embedded within a larger plan for addressing the structural roots of conflict and the search for durable and inclusive political settlements to disputes (Berdal 2019: 115).

Based on a broader definition of stabilization missions, De Coning (2018: 97) argues that these operations should ideally combine military action with political, humanitarian and development initiatives among different UN and regional actors, so contributing to delineate and set in motion long-lasting structural solutions to political, economic and social conflicts. In order to be sustainable in the long term, these contingency force operations should best only focus on one initial phase of intervention and later limit their obligations through division of work and partnering with other UN agencies and regional organizations, transferring demanding follow-on tasks to competent partners in the field of humanitarian and development cooperation for a long-term reconstruction plan (of at least ten years) – and particularly, rebuilding and training the host nation security sector to transfer defense and public order functions to local army and police (Berdal/Ucko 2015: 9, De Coning 2018: 91, Berdal 2019: 126). Simultaneously, in the political arena, UN special envoys and mediators are needed "to take special steps to simultaneously increase the political pressure on the government to address legitimate political grievances and to invest in the extension of state authority, including the provision of basic services, justice, and law and order" and ensuring inclusiveness and representation in the political realm (De Coning 2018: 96–97).

In a nutshell, the use of force by UN peace operations is the outcome of an evolutionary process in peacekeeping and conflict management practices, mirroring an adaptation to both the nature of conflicts and their challenges, as well as the capability of the international community to address them. In practice, the use of coercive force by stabilization missions raises some critical issues, which bring to light the inherent strengths and shortcomings associated to this kind of complex undertakings, namely: the ambiguity of the mandate, the tension with the principle of impartiality by peace operations, the disposal of required operative and tactical capabilities, the negative unintended consequences of using force, and its ultimate purpose as a means to peacebuilding. These five critical issues serve as the analytical framework for addressing the experiences in this matter for the selected case study, as drawn in section 4 of this paper – after first delivering a brief characterization of the underlying Haitian political and social context.

3 Haiti: A Long-Standing Failed State

3.1 Brief Socio-Political Overview of Haiti

Simply put, "Haiti's socio-political history is a tapestry of revolution, turmoil, dictatorship, intermittent attempts at democracy, and near state collapse" (Tindi/Agwanda/Nyadera 2024: 328). For more than three centuries (1492–1804), Haiti was under Spanish and French colonial rule as a prosperous sugarcane colony, until it gained independence following the Haitian Revolution (1791–1804) under the leadership of the two national heroes, Toussaint Louverture and Jean-Jacques Dessalines, thus becoming the first freed slave nation in the world. During the 19th century and mid-20th century, Haiti experienced a period of high political instability and economic stagnation, including constant coups d'état and popular rebellions, intermittent political conflict between the north and south of the country, repeated constitutional changes and the oscillation of the political system among parliamentarian republics and absolute monarchies, a long political and armed conflict with neighboring Dominican Republic, and 20-year occupation by the United States (cf. Girard 2010). The country's (forced) political stabilization occurred under the totalitarian and ruthless dictatorship of the Duvalier family (1957–1986), which comprised the reign of terror and state-sponsored violence by the father-and-son duo François and Jean-Claude Duvalier (known as *Papa* and *Baby Doc*, respectively).

Haiti's path to democratic transition started with the election of the priest Jean-Bertrand Aristide in 1990 and his pro-democracy movement *Lavalas* (the flood, in Haitian Creole). Aristide's early attempts to carry out modest but substantive social, economic and political-administrative reforms caused fierce opposition from the old business and military elites, which ultimately led to a coup d'état in September 1991 and the reinstatement of military rule for three years. Following international mediation and pressure, Aristide returned to power in 1994, this time with a more radical reform program supported by the international community – which included the disbandment of the Haitian armed forces due to their dark history of human rights abuses and involvement in coups, and he later handed over power democratically to his political ally, the agronomist René Préval (1996–2001), who attempted to set in motion a liberal program of economic adjustment and privatization.

This paved the way for Aristide's reelection (2001–2004), whose return to power was marked by highly confrontational politics, poor governance, widespread corruption and links to drug trafficking networks – until he was ousted again amid a widespread political crisis and armed uprising by an allegedly US-backed coup d'état, followed by a transitional government of technocrats under Boniface Alexandre as president and Gérard Latortue as prime minister (2004–2006). Since then, although political power has been passed on peacefully through elections, contemporary Haitian politics over the last twenty years has been plagued by the same persistent political and economic mismanagement, high fragmentation of the party landscape – whose members lack common agreement and are at odds with each other; clientelism, corruption and patronage among high-ranking officials, embezzlement and linkage with organized crime, recurring political turmoil and social unrest, and a series of devastating natural disasters such as hurricanes, floods and earthquakes.

The greatest natural disaster occurred during Préval's second term (2006–2011): On 12 January 2010, a 7.0 earthquake hit Port-au-Prince, causing the almost complete destruction of state institutions' facilities, "the death of an estimated 230,000 people, rendered 1.3 million people homeless and led to an estimated loss of between USD 7 to 14 billion, a loss far exceeding the GDP of the country" (Tindi/Agwanda/Nyadera 2024: 329). International aid for the reconstruction of the country amounted to USD 9.9 billion pledges in donations and credits and was managed by the Interim Haiti Recovery Commission (IHRC) in partnership with the Haitian government and foreign donors. In reality, this aid materialized little into effective reconstruction and improvement in the quality of life of Haitians, partly due to a slow pace of disbursement of the assistance money, corruption, lack of coordination and tensions between Haitian and international members of the IHRC, a lack of legitimacy in its work and poor implementation of approved projects (Lundahl 2013: 250–256).

The discontent of Haitians with a flawed post-earthquake reconstruction and mismanagement of funds paved the way for the election of the entrepreneur and *konpa* singer Michel Martelly (2011–2016), who amid a vague and populist election campaign, promised to launch an overarching process of national refoundation. In practice, Martelly's administration was marked by the same old vices: poor governance, cabinet turnovers, state capture for private purposes, economic malfeasance and ties to organized crime, which led to his forced resignation in February 2016. The subsequent and contested elections in November 2016 – the latest ones held so far – brought the ruling party's candidate to the presidency, Jovenel Moïse (2017–2021), whose term in office characterized by the advance of an authoritarian presidentialist rule, high political instability, a deep economic downturn, de facto standstill in state administration due to lack of funding, several waves of popular unrest demanding his resignation and an attempted coup.

Since 2021, the country has been plunged into a deep and widespread political, social and economic collapse with no point of return: On 7 July 2021, President Moïse was shot dead while sleeping at his private residence by hired Colombian mercenaries, and a month later, on 14 August 2021, Haiti was struck again by a 7.2 earthquake at the Department Sud, that left almost 3,000 people dead and more than 12,000 injured. In particular, political governance has been particularly challenging since then, as the interim government under prime minister Ariel Henry (2021–2024) ruled with the backup of foreign powers but was perceived as illegitimate by much of the population and political opposition, largely because of his reluctance to call general elections and share power with other state branches. This is the by-product of structural flaws in the country's political governance, since "there has been no election of any sort since 2016 [as no electoral commission is currently in office nor there is an up-to-date voter register], and the parliament has not held a session since January 2020, when the terms of all the deputies in the lower house and almost all the senators expired. The country's remaining elected officials – a rump bloc of ten senators – saw their terms run out in January 2023" (ICG 2024: 4).

Political agreement among Haitian political forces that helped pave the way toward a political transition was achieved under the mediation of the Caribbean Community (Caricom) in Jamaica in March 2024, leading to Henry's resignation and the installation of a nine-member Transitional Presidential Council (TPC) a month later. This council, composed of nine members – seven voting members from the main political party coalitions and the private sector, and two non-voting observers from civil society – and with a rotating chair, currently under the businessman Laurent Saint-Cyr, is tasked with paving the political-institutional path for transferring power to elected officials by 7 February 2026. For this purpose, the TPC was given the daunting task of reforming the still-in-force 1987 Constitution and organizing a general election. While rewriting the post-Duvalier constitution is a cornerstone for reshaping the country's political system and its central institutions, and fostering more effective governance, the council decided in October 2025 to halt consultations for drafting a new constitution and cancel the planned referendum, arguing that "the country cannot afford another divisive political experiment while Haitians are demanding basic security and essential services, and holding such a referendum is now seen as an obstacle to the ongoing electoral process" (Blaise 2025a). As a fallback, the TPC has devoted its efforts to calling general elections to choose a new president and renewing the bicameral National Assembly – however, this endeavor faces serious logistical and security challenges. With few financial resources available, a lack of electoral agency's technical staff and an updated electoral register, around 15% of the population internally displaced and the same percentage living abroad, and the incapacity to set up polling stations in areas under gang control, it is highly doubtful whether the Haitian state will be able to actually hold elections that meet the standards of legality and universality (ICG 2025: 8–9). Although the TPC has moved forward with its goal and already issued an electoral decree outlining the rules for future polls, the Provisional Electoral Council declared it "materially impossible" under the current circumstances due to the prevailing violence and lack of funds, estimated at USD 137 million (Blaise 2025b).

Since the Transitional Presidential Council's mandate cannot be in theory extended, the risk of a power vacuum and unclear political outlook for the country for 2026 raise enormous uncertainties and questions about the country's near fate, as well as whether the fledgling governance apparatus in place can cope over the short and medium term with the main threat to the existence of the state and social order: the criminal gangs.

3.2 The Gangs: Haiti's Old yet Latest Scourge

Haiti has a long trajectory of non-state armed groups of a paramilitary, para-police and criminal nature that, due to weak state consolidation and a tradition of authoritarian rule, have long existed under various forms and with different principals. Not only was the independence war fought by paramilitary bands, but as a result of persistent state dysfunctionality, its weak presence throughout the territory and a security vacuum, a series of groups (such as militias, death squads, criminal gangs and vigilantes) have flourished over time coexisting alongside the formal state security agencies and in many cases been promoted and sponsored by the ruling political elites for the purpose of gaining and maintaining political power. Thus, these non-state armed groups are "neither clearly enemies nor clearly allies of the Haitian state – nor, indeed, clearly distinct from it. [...] They [are], in other words, typical of the kind of mixed state/non-state, political-criminal networked spoilers that contemporary peace operations and peacebuilders must confront, especially in urban settings" (Cockayne 2014: 738).

Traditionally, Haitian non-state armed groups of a criminal nature have been used and misused by local politicians and business elites as tools for self-protection, political competition and warfare, and exercise of social control and oppression over the population, mainly against residents of Port-au-Prince *bidonvilles* (shantytowns). Consequently, Haitian gangs "have long been hired as thugs and played an important role in the country's clientelistic networks as intermediaries between local communities, politicians and businesspeople" (Schuberth 2015: 174). Sadly, "this is how Haiti 'works', as a violent system of competition for 'protection' between fluid alliances of political, criminal, military and business factions, tied together in diverse networks, whose internal alliances' power-centers may shift imperceptibly" (Cockayne 2014: 739). However, these actors do not solely serve as instruments of political and economic power struggles, but during downturn periods in request for their violent services, "gangs appear to resort to two alternative sources of income: either they increase their collaboration with organized crime groups, or they extract resources from their own communities" (Schuberth 2015: 171).

Haitian criminal gangs trace their origins to the second half of the 20th century. During the Duvalier era, irregular militias were formally created as a tool for coup-proofing, repressing dissent and exercising systematic state terror, known as *Tonton Makout* (the gunnysack uncle or boogeyman, in Haitian Creole), a savage death squad that carried out tens of thousands of politically motivated executions, beatings, kidnappings, sexual assaults and disappearances, even in broad daylight. After the fall of the Duvalier dynasty, the *Tonton Makout* were never formally disbanded, they but instead became mercenary groups at the service of several principals – mainly politicians and criminals – who demanded and paid for their criminal services. Thence, Haitian gangs have been "readily available for the one who would offer the big money, irrespective of any ideological conviction. [...] Urban gangs have repeatedly switched from one political side to the other, depending on which party remunerates them most generously" (Schuberth 2015: 180). Consequently, after the Duvalier era, a kind of intertwining among politics, crime and gangs emerged, whereby Haiti's political and economic elite have informally contracted these groups to protect them, but at the same time no clear distinction between political and criminal patrons exists, since many top public office-holders once started their career as gang leaders or have repeatedly been involved in transnational criminal activities supported by gangs.

Under Aristide, the militia phenomenon and its link to politics reached a peak, as a large number of newly armed non-state actors flourished, either opposing or supporting him and the ruling party, *Fanmi Lavalas*. On one side, Aristide abolished the Haitian armed forces in 1995 in response to its long history of human rights abuses and involvement in coups, but without a real program of disarmament, demobilization and reintegration for its members. This caused many former military personnel turned into irregular militias – collectively called the "rebel army", which began engaging in warfare against the state in the northern and eastern parts of the country and in criminal activities in general – like black market economy, extortion, kidnappings and drug trafficking – as alternative income sources (Kolbe 2013: 3–4). On the other side, Aristide formally sponsored new urban vigilante gangs as coup-proofing groups and for the enforcement of social order and intimidation of the opposition, the so-called *chimès* (monster or ghost, in Haitian Creole) organized in *baz* (bases or neighborhoods): long-established grassroots community organizations engaged in local governance (Girard 2010: 185–187). In exchange for protection, the *chimès* received monthly payments from the payroll of state-owned companies, weapons and protecttion from being arrested by the police (Schuberth 2015: 180) – although Aristide slowly lost control over them, which became serious perpetrators of indiscriminate violence and even a threat to himself.

After Aristide's forced departure from power in 2004, the *chimès* went out of control after losing their main sponsor and embarked on a predatory war of survival and terror against the state and common citizens through armed attacks, robberies, kidnappings, gender-based violence, extortion of merchants and drivers, and contract killings. Due to their violent actions noneffectively countered by a weak state security apparatus, these groups managed to consolidate their control and authority in the largest and poorest neighborhoods of Port-au-Prince – until they were significantly dammed up as a result of gang-clearing operations launched between 2004 and 2007 by MINUSTAH (see following section).

Since the 2010s, a transformation of the Haitian gangs' main sponsors, motivations and raison d'être has occurred following a process of acute political, social and economic collapse of the country, which can be traced to the 2010 earthquake and the flawed subsequent reconstruction process, and the political crisis opened after President Moïse's assassination in 2021 (Tindi/ Agwanda/Nyadera 2024: 329–330). As a result, two new distinctive traits arose in the trajectory of these groups: On the one hand, their patrons and sponsors became less political in nature and are now mainly linked to transnational organized crime. In a political dimension, the Préval administration engaged in negotiations with the gangs to stop their campaign of violence, while the governments of Martinelly and Moïse, although occasionally instrumentalized the gangs to do the dirty job of suppressing political opposition and keeping social control during episodes of social unrest, they did not establish a strong and abiding patronage relationship with the gangs as observed before (Schuberth 2015: 181, Harvard Law School International Human Rights Clinic 2021: 7–15). Conversely, transnational organized crime became the new patrons and principals of gangs, mainly those linked to the international trafficking of cocaine and marijuana from Haiti to the United States, stemming mainly from Colombia and Venezuela – and recently, cases of child and organ trafficking have been also reported (Blaise 2025c, Francisque 2025, BINUH 2025b: 14). Likewise, well-established Haitian criminal cells operating in the United States, Dominican Republic and Jamaica have become strategic allies of the gangs to make profitable their businesses related to these trafficking activities, as well as the provision of weapons, tactical training, contact networks and logistical support (Le Cour/Oliveira/ Herbert 2024: 14, Wakefield/Giles/Cheetham 2025).

On the other hand, gangs have acquired both structure (similar to drug mafias, cartels and militias) and a degree of autonomy, becoming self-sufficient actors that essentially mobilize to achieve their own economic interests and social leverage for their members – particularly those of the gang leaders themselves. The transformation of contemporary Haitian gangs is exemplarily illustrated by a statement of one Haitian entrepreneur and local politician: "We saw a lion being born, we fed it and watched it grow, we tried to domesticate it, but the animal eventually escaped from the cage" (quoted by Le Cour/Oliveira/Herbert 2024: 4). Consequently, "over the past five years, gangs have undergone a radical evolution, going from rather unstructured actors dependent on resources provided by public or private patronage to violent entrepreneurs who have been able to convert their territorial power into governance capabilities" (ibid.: 3).

Contemporary Haitian gangs comprise an estimated of more than 200 cells made from a dozen men up to 2,000 members, mainly operating over 85% of Port-au-Prince metropolitan area – including the communes of Cité Soleil, Delmas, Tabarre, Carrefour and Pétionville – and the Artibonite and Central departments, where much of the country's food is grown (Le Cour/ Oliveira/Herbert 2024: 6, BINUH 2025a). Thus, they operate in an interconnected way both in urban and rural areas, are organized vertically around strong gang leaders, who count on extensive influential networks that provide them with funding, weapons and connections with corrupt state authorities and mafia bosses, and whose actions comprise a broad repertoire of violent and criminal enterprises (see Table 1). Their activities are basically criminal-extractive and targeted against rival gangs, state security forces and common citizens for purposes of territorial, resources and social control, including plundering, extortion, kidnapping, village massacres, murder, forced displacement, the domination or destruction of critical infrastructure such as commercial and oil port terminals, bridges and major road nodes; and restriction of freedom of movement through checkpoints and protection racket.

Determinant of typology	Characteristic
Location	*Urban* / mostly found in Haiti's 'popular zones' and operate in distinct territories *Rural* / Peri-urban operations not linked to one specific territory
Nature of operations	*Village* / neighborhood policing *Informal* territorial governance *Criminal* / Extortion, kidnapping, looting
Leadership	*Hierarchical* *Individual* with a following of trusted armed henchmen
Origin	*Former members* of militias and the defunct Haitian army Groups from *poor neighborhoods*
Vertical structure of authority	*Answerable to political and economic elites* who fund their activities *Answerable to the group leader*

Table 1: Typology of contemporary criminal gangs in Haiti
Source: Tindi/Agwanda/Nyadera (2024: 332)

One of the most striking expressions of the brutality of violence deployed by these gangs is the use of sexual violence against women and girls as a central practice of social control, as "some gangs have authorized their soldiers to carry out mass rapes, an instrument of terror that also serves to discipline populations. In certain cases, rapes are committed in public, in front of large groups of civilians, or even the victims' families" (Le Cour/Oliveira/Herbert 2024: 18). Between May and August 2025 alone, 2,646 cases of sexual assaults were reported, of which collective rape accounted for 85% of cases (BINUH 2025b: 9–10). In response to this and other forms of indiscriminate gang violence, grassroot vigilante self-defense and justice brigades have flourished, known as *Bwa kale* (peeled wood, in Haitian Creole, in allusion to the sharpened wooden sticks and machetes used by their members) to deter gangs from entering their neighborhoods and hunt down the bandits by committing extrajudicial killings through mob lynching (ICG 2024: 8). *Bwa kale* "might be best understood as a renewed set of old practices of community surveillance and patrolling that intersect with neighborhood 'brigades' and '*baz*' [... and] as a fluid 'mob' response that can be activated in specific circumstances, such as gang attacks. [...] At the core of *Bwa kale* lies the citizens' will to restore order and security, take justice into their own hands, and punish enemies – gang members or not – through physical violence. The latter includes public lynching and executions, of which more than 600 cases have been registered since April 2023, according to local sources" (Le Cour/ Oliveira/Herbert 2024: 14). These actions take place on a very small territorial scale with support, permissiveness and even participation from police officers – who "can therefore perform their public duty, in uniform, during one part of the day, before becoming a vigilante, dressed as a civilian, during another" (ibid.: 15).

In brief, the ongoing conflict in Haiti stems from a protracted power struggle among gangs and the state's incapacity to cope with them. On the one side, since 2021, Port-au-Prince has been the battlefield of a brutal confrontation for dominance between two gang federations: *Fòs Revolisyonè G9 an Fanmi e Alye* (Revolutionary Forces of the G9 Family and Allies, known as G9), led by the former police officer Jimmy Chérizier (alias Barbecue) and connected to the former ruling party, the *Parti Haïtien Tèt Kale*; and its rival, *G-Pèp*, headed by Jean-Pierre Gabriel (alias Ti Gabriel) and broadly supported by Haitian opposition parties (Mistler-Ferguson 2022). In February 2024, these two gang coalitions put aside their squabbles and formed a grand alliance, called *Viv Ansanm* (living together, in Haitian Creole) with Chérizier as maximum leader. The building of this alliance marked a striking shift in the gangs' patterns of violence, as they joined forces and launched a crusade against the state as part of a self-proclaimed "political mission" to "break Haiti's oligarchs hold on power" by attacking strategic locations such as police stations, prisons, main seaports, the international airport, the presidential palace and other public buildings (ICG 2025: 14). Moreover, *Viv Ansanm* works as a brand for recruitment of new members and further territorial expansion through franchising, by integrating new small and local cells within the alliance's protection network – although de facto this coalition is still somewhat loose, with tensions and occasional clashes occurring within different blocs (Le Cour/Oliveira/Herbert 2024: 10–12).

On the other side, the proliferation and strengthening of criminal gangs is also a byproduct of a process of profound state collapse. Following Moïse's assassination, Haiti has become politically ungovernable, with a breakdown in state authority and its capacity to exert an effective monopoly on legitimate violence. This deterioration has been acutely evident in the condition of the Haitian National Police (PNH, by its French acronym), the main agency responsible for maintaining public order and law enforcement. The PNH suffer from chronic institutional weakness and incapacity to meet the challenge posed by gangs on their own. Although on paper, the PNH number 13,501 officers (BINUH 2025b: 5), the real force strength is estimated to around 3,300 active policemen, as the institution is plagued by desertion, indiscipline, insubordination, corruption and even collusion with the gangs (ICG 2024: 5). Due to the state's bankruptcy, which prevents it from paying salaries or allocating the financial resources needed to make public agencies functional, police stations are dilapidated and lack the personnel and equipment required to respond operationally and tactically to gang activities – which have recently exacerbated their attacks against PNH personnel and police posts and stations. While most police personnel are engaged in patrol duties, the Haitian Coast Guard and Border Police are chronically understaffed, and as a result, maritime and air borders are virtually uncontrolled, facilitating the illegal smuggling of weapons and goods (Le Cour/Oliveira/ Herbert 2024: 21). Alongside this, as a means of economic survival, some defected policemen and ex-soldiers have engaged in freelance services by providing trainings in special tactics to gangs' members, so enhancing their operational capability to confront police during assaults on stations and outposts and street combat (ibid.: 13)

Haiti's state collapse and insecurity situation caused by gangs' actions have opened a spiral of violence that tears society apart and costs human lives every day. As is often the case in scenarios where the social fabric breaks down, widespread violence erupts, and law enforcement and justice delivery are nearly absent, it is virtually impossible to accurately estimate the total number of victims and fatalities in the country, but overall figures account for more than 16,000 people killed and some 7,000 injured in armed violence since 1 January 2022 (OHCHR 2025). Between July and September 2025 alone, 1,247 people were murdered and 710 injured by gangs (30%), self-defense groups and mobs under the context of *Bwa kale* actions (9%), and during security force operations against gangs, including summary executions and civilian casualties (61%). In addition, 398 women and girls were victims of sexual violence, 145 people were kidnapped and at least 1,400,000 people are estimated to be internally displaced (BINUH 2025c: 3, 5).

On balance, this brief characterization accounts for two overlapping processes in Haiti's political and social governance for more than three decades. On the one hand, there is a long-lasting process of state deterioration and collapse from above, due to authoritarian politics, flawed democratic transition, poor governance, mismanagement, state capture and corruption practices. On the other hand, and largely as a byproduct of the above factors, the gangs have been a permanent player in the social structure and configuration of political power in Haiti from the bottom. These actors have emerged as grassroots tools for the creation and maintenance of political and social order – originally as proxies for the political and economic elites, now as autonomous players with their own agendas and interests and a high degree of power and influence due to a state vacuum.

4 The Use of Force in Haiti

Given this turbulent backdrop of deep-rooted social and political instability, it is not surprising that the international community has become actively engaged in Haiti to prevent a total state collapse and support the co-management of internal conflict – as a result, the country has hosted the largest number of peace operations in the entire history of UN peacekeeping (see Table 2): 13 in total, ranging from transitional observation and monitoring missions, interim multinational forces, security and justice sector reform missions, special political missions for mediation and advise, and stabilization operations.

Timeframe	Operation
1993–1996	UN Mission in Haiti (UNMIH)
1993–2000	UN-OAS International Civilian Mission in Haiti (MICIVIH)
1994–1995	US-led Multinational Force (MNF)
1996–1997	UN Support Mission in Haiti (UNSMIH)
1997	UN Transition Mission in Haiti (UNTMIH)
1997–2000	UN Civilian Police Mission in Haiti (MIPONUH)
2000–2001	International Civilian Support Mission in Haiti (MICAH)
2004	Multinational Interim Force (MIF)
2004–2017	UN Stabilization Mission in Haiti (MINUSTAH)
2017–2019	UN Mission for Justice Support in Haiti (MINUJUSTH)
2019–today	United Nations Integrated Office in Haiti (BINUH)
2023–2025	Multinational Security Support Mission in Haiti (MSS)
2025–ongoing	Gang Suppression Force (GSF)

Table 2: United Nations Peace Operations in Haiti
Source: own elaboration

In this work, MINUSTAH and MSS are selected as samples for an in-depth examination because they constitute the only two operations among those listed above that have been mandated by the Security Council under Chapter VII of the UN Charta to deal with threats to international peace and security, and therefore, authorized to use coercive force to cope with armed non-state actors for stabilization purposes and uphold state authority, while the protection of civilians and support for overall statebuilding have been subsidiary aims. This analysis – drawn on the five critical issues outlined in section 2 – will provide detailed insight into prior experiences of UN engagement in Haiti by critically revisiting the implementation of the use of force doctrine in stabilization missions, its strengths and pitfalls, to later deliver an outlook and a set of future recommendations for the newly launched GSF.

4.1   The United Nations Stabilization Mission in Haiti

The UN Stabilization Mission in Haiti (MINUSTAH, by its French acronym) was the first ever UN stabilization mission and the longest and largest peace operation to date in the history of its engagement with Haiti: lasting 13 years (from June 2004 to October 2017), composed at its peak of 2,366 soldiers and 2,374 police officers – from 19 countries in total, under the command of Brazil – and 304 international civilian personnel. Set up by UNSC Resolution 1542 on 30 April 2004 to address and manage the social chaos unleashed after Aristide's forced departure from power, MINUSTAH's stabilization mandate is quite extensive and comprises two dimensions: on the one hand, ensuring, through its military component and all available capabilities, a secure and stable environment, the extension of state authority throughout Haiti and the restoration and upholding of the rule of law and public order to enable the resumption of a political and constitutional process; and, on the other, the reform, reorganization and training of the PNH as well as the disarmament, demobilization and reintegration of armed non-state actors by the police and civilian component.

It follows that the mandate given to MINUSTAH, while quite ambitious in its aims of stabilizing the country and restoring government authority and social order, lacks clarity regarding the means and boundaries. Therefore, MINUSTAH was entrusted in loose and diffuse terms with broad goals under a clear security-first approach, only stipulating in a short but vague sentence that the mission could use all its capabilities to achieve them – without expressly authorizing the use of coercive force. This instance is emblematic of a certain caution within the UNSC in the early 2000s to openly mention in its resolutions about consent to use force for stabilization purposes under Chapter VII powers, while leaving the door open to every possible option, which De Coning (2008: 87) refers to as "constructive ambiguity."

Owing to a severe deterioration in the security situation in the country and the credibility of the mission to address it after its first year of deployment, MINUSTAH "saw the introduction of new practices within the context of a UN peace operation, namely the use of joint military-police forces to conduct offensive action against armed groups that were labelled as 'gangs'" (Pingeot 2018: 365), and therefore, decided to embark in late 2004 in gang-clearing operations to counter the *chimès* and rural militias through employing high-intensity lethal force. This the consequence of the uncompromising stance by the Préval government, which after failed attempts at negotiation declared that "the gangs must 'disarm or die'," thus giving the green light for the Haitian army and police to launch an armed campaign of extermination against gang leaders and to take back control of gang-held areas by force (Dorn 2018: 129, Cockayne 2014: 750). MINUSTAH joined these endeavors in a combative stance by conducting a series of air and ground military raids in Port-au-Prince shantytowns (above all in Cité Soleil and Bel Air), taking place between 2004 and 2007, which actually became the very core of the mission's activities (Dorn 2009: 818). These operations clearly positioned MINUSTAH in a warring position against gangs as targeted enemies, which is the outcome of a criminalization of the Haitian conflict caused by a discursive shift from politically motivated to criminally motivated violence (Schuberth 2015: 177), as the gangs became "a threat to the stability of the Haitian state, and therefore to broader international peace and security – and MINUSTAH simply adapted to this reality [...] in a context of simultaneous wars 'on terror' and 'on drugs'" (Pingeot 2018: 367). Consequently, under new discourses on the international arena after 9–11 and a crime-conflict nexus approach for UN peacekeeping practices, the labelling of the gangs as peace and security aggressors altered MINUSTAH practices of intervention, and legitimized its loss of neutrality relative to the Haitian conflict parties and the adoption of militarized approaches to deal with the gangs through the use of coercive force (ibid.: 368).

MINUSTAH engaged in a relatively successful manner in these high-intensity counter-gang operations, largely because it enjoyed vigorous political and financial support from UN headquarters, as well as operative and tactical capabilities in-situ after a significant increase in the mission's strength and the creation of a "rapid reaction force" to more effectively ensure public security and order, particularly in and around Port-au-Prince (UNSC Resolution 1608 on 22 June 2005). Following an initial phase with substantial operational, tactical and strategic flaws, MINUSTAH achieved in a quick and short period of time to build and put together a well-equipped, competently led, well-integrated and highly capable multinational forces, particularly from the Brazilian contingent, that included many officers with broad experience and know-how in dealing with criminal gangs in the favelas (Cockayne 2014: 746). During these raids, MINUSTAH made use of a wide range of resources in a coordinated manner to maximize the effectiveness of operations and minimize damage, including the combination of aerial and infantry power, transversal coordination and integration between police and military components, the use of combined instruments of intervention comprising military raids together with strong law enforcement powers by Formed Police Units, the use of diversionary tactics to create confusion among the gangs, the employment of night vision and infrared capabilities, snipers and unmanned aerial vehicles to drop leaflets warning civilians of the impending attack, the integration of PNH squads for providing assistance through cordon and crowd control, and the establishment of safe corridors for Red Cross mobile units to assist the wounded (Cockayne 2014: 754, Pingeot 2018: 376–378, Dorn 2018: 134–136).

Key to the fruitful planning, management and conduct of counter-gang operations in Cité Soleil and Bel Air was the development of a comprehensive and multilayered mission's intelligence capability through human and technological assets. Over time, MINUSTAH evolved to a well-planned, focused and limited use of force by the adoption of criminal investigation techniques through a Joint Mission Analysis Cell (JMAC), which by making use of generated human intelligence through a network of local informants allowed for a careful preparation of operations. The intelligence furnished by the JMAC – in support of the PNH – relied heavily on treating the local population as key terrain for gaining key data through a toll-free 24/7 hotline to confidentially share information on gang routine activities, and a paid network of local informants (Dorn 2009: 821–822). Largely, "MINUSTAH was also able to purchase information, in part because the inhabitants of Haiti's *bidonvilles* are so poor that the price of such information was low enough to be within the very limited means available to the JMAC, and below the level that would have triggered political scrutiny and interference from its backers" (Cockayne 2014: 760). Likewise, the JMAC substantially developed with appropriate technological tools highly valuable imagery intelligence via aerial photography of defensive trenches, resupply and repair positions, weapons caches, stores of loot, command headquarters, sleeping locations and escape routes, which allowed a better preparation of the battlespace and running of operations (Dorn 2009: 823–824). Besides these operational measures, MINUSTAH also pioneered the institutionalization of intelligence structures within the mission headquarters and nationally, in tandem with the regional battalions of the national contingents, but also externally by liaising closely with the UN operations center and collection analysis units (ibid.: 830–831).

On balance, these raids were successful in neutralizing and arresting a large number of gang leaders, as well as retaking their centers of control and operations within the Port-au-Prince slums, causing the gangs' structures and support bases to collapse (Cockayne 2014: 753). However, these operations also brought with them negative unintended consequences, such as collateral damage: During the anti-gang raids, there were a large number of casualties among gang members and civilians, which casted shadows over the proper observance of the mission's rules of engagement while deploying disproportionate and undifferentiated lethal violence, but also raised broader concerns on the legal responsibility by MINUSTAH in committing extrajudicial and summary executions. Since many operations were conducted "during sleeping hours in residential slums, cobbled together from corrugated iron, wood and even cardboard, through which munitions passed with great ease and harmed civilians" (Cockayne 2014: 747–748). The ultimate expression of these raids was Operation Iron Fist in July 2005, where about 1,400 heavily armed military and police peacekeepers entered Cité Soleil to conduct a 12-hour anti-gang raid, firing 22,700 rounds of ammunition and 78 grenades, leaving over 30 civilians dead and injuring dozens, most of them elderly, women and children (Pingeot 2018: 366). Although it is plausible – as argued by MINUSTAH spokespersons – that some civilian casualties occurred in revenge by the gangs in retaliation for tactical assistance and collaboration provided to MINUSTAH forces by slum dwellers (Dorn 2018: 128), witnesses and victims' relatives have attested to mission's responsibility for these accidental killings – for which no blame was ever publicly acknowledged, prosecution pursued or any form of reparation and compensation were made (cf. Wills/McLaughin 2017); and these actions fueled public discourse that MINUSTAH was behaving de facto as a "foreign occupation force," thus causing social protests against the mission in Haiti's urban centers (Cockayne 2014: 748). Furthermore, as a byproduct, these actions resulted in greater vulnerability for the security and safety of UN personnel, since MINUSTAH military and civilian personnel became a bull's-eye for gang attacks, particularly on public roads through "fire and run" tactics (Dorn 2018: 128).

Although the balance of MINUSTAH stabilization objectives was positive, the mission was also given a political mandate to support the restoration of political and constitutional order and promote national dialogue and reconciliation by providing technical, logistical, and administrative assistance for the conduct of elections, and fostering good governance and institutional development at the local levels. Less effort was devoted to these areas because MINUSTAH activities between 2004 and 2010 focused mainly on security issues through gang-clearing operations in Port-au-Prince slums, which in the long term did not help to enhance and strengthen state presence and capacity in a sustainable way, since they were not matched by a re-insertion of Haitian state to hold the territories in the long term, as efforts to restructure the social, economic and political structures of the country were rather marginal. In the judgment of many local and international critics, MINUSTAH failed in coupling the use of force with a larger project for Haitian political and economic transformation, as the mission's approach "through a security lens appeared misguided, as security issues were inter-twined with equally important political and economic grievances. In this con-text, MINUSTAH responded only to the symptoms of violence, rather than to its causes" (Lemay-Hébert 2015: 722–723). Although MINUSTAH invested some efforts in repairing the damage done to the neighborhoods during com-bat operations and providing socio-economic assistance at local levels in the form of Quick Impact Programs to restore physical infrastructure and provide access to basic public goods and services, such as food, water, medical services, sport and education, or via community violence reduction initiatives to create economic and social alternatives to divert gang members from violence (Cockayne 2014: 763, Lemay-Hébert 2015: 726, Dorn 2018: 133), it lacked a comprehensive long-term statebuilding and economic recovery plan, in articulation with other relevant UN agencies.

Furthermore, although MINUSTAH succeeded in breaking up the gangs and enabled the Haitian government to regain control of the capital (Dorn 2018: 132) – so thus achieving its operational objective, the political aim of dismantling the linkage between the gangs and the Haitian political-business elites and the existence of local structures of power that sustained hybrid governance structures remained somewhat unarticulated and elusive, and perhaps ultimately unfeasible (Cockayne 2014: 738, Lemay-Hébert 2015: 723). Even, it may be argued that MINUSTAH actions just "amounted to a strategy of 'containment' rather than a real political solution of the Haitian conflict" (Pingeot 2018: 379) and rather contributed to reinforcing the logic of confrontation at play between the Haitian state and society (Lemay-Hébert 2015: 724).

And as the underlying roots of social and political conflict were never substantially addressed, when the devastating 2010 earthquake occurred and flawed internationally-led reconstruction followed, the achievements gained in countering the gangs were thrown away as they flourished again with greater force against a collapsed state capacity, distorted economy and an even more impoverished and vulnerable population. The post-earthquake period also marks a second moment in the course of MINUSTAH until its closure in 2017. The mission was dismantled and decapitated internally during the disaster – with 102 casualties, including the death of the Head of

Mission and Chief of Joint Command – and its tasks shifted to focus more on supporting immediate recovery, humanitarian aid delivery, basic infrastructure reconstruction, and the provision of public order under the umbrella of the IHRC (2010–2012). Later, the mission lost both local support – as a result of a series of scandals involving sexual exploitation and abuse of minors by UN peacekeepers mainly from Sri Lanka, Pakistan and Uruguay; and the outbreak of cholera in October 2010 caused by a pathogen introduced by Nepali peacekeepers, killing more than 8,000 people and affecting over 670,000 (Lemay-Hébert 2015: 725, The Independent 2017) – as well as political and diplomatic backing at UN headquarters, now focused on newly-launched integrated stabilization missions in Africa. Thus, the mission began its exit strategy with a gradual reduction of authorized personnel in 2013, finally handing over the flag in April 2017 to a smaller, lower-profile successor mission, the UN Mission for Justice Support in Haiti (MINUJUSTH).

4.2 The Multinational Security Support Mission in Haiti

Seven years after MINUSTAH withdrawal, on 2 October 2023, the UNSC launched the Multinational Security Support Mission in Haiti (MSS) to address the crisis unleashed in the country since 2021 as a result of the exacerbation of the state collapse triggered by the assassination of President Moïse, the rapid expansion of urban gangs and the escalation of violence. The question of why the UN responded so late to the severe situation in Haiti is answered by the blockage within the Security Council due to geopolitical conflicts and escalating tensions among P–5 members following the Russian aggression war against Ukraine and the conspicuous reluctance by the United States, France and Brazil to once again engage actively and providing leadership and troops to an international peace support mission in Haiti (Tindi/Agwanda/Nyaburi 2024: 322).

The MSS was a non-conventional peace mission – namely, an ad hoc coalition of states rather than a traditional UN-led blue-helmeted operation – lasting a year and a half (from January 2024 to October 2025), led by Kenya and made of a contingent of 991 officers mainly from the Kenyan National Police Service (three-quarters of the total) and by soldiers and military police from the Bahamas, Belize, Guatemala, El Salvador and Jamaica. Established by UNSC Resolution 2699 under Chapter VII powers, MSS mandate provided support to the PNH in the planning and conduct of joint security operations to counter gangs – as well as protecting critical state infrastructure, transit points and humanitarian aid delivery, and combatting illicit arms trafficking – with the aims of improving the security situation in Haiti and creating the conditions conducive to holding free and fair elections in the short term, while promoting the country's long-term institutional, social and economic development and sustainable stability. To achieve these aims, the UNCS authorized the MSS expressly to take all necessary measures to fulfil its mandate, provided that these are limited in scope, time-bound, proportionate and consistent with international human rights law.

From the above it follows that the UNSC enabled the MSS – as did with MINUSTAH – in vague terms to engage in coercive measures involving the use of force under the umbrella of Chapter VII powers to fulfill its clear but ambitious mandate: backing up the Haitian police in protecting state institutions and critical infrastructure and launching a counter-offensive against gangs, in order to stabilize the security situation and lay the foundations for a process of restoring political order by holding democratic elections (ICG 2024: 11). Therefore, as MINUSTAH, the MSS was assembled around a security-centered and warrying narrative focused on fighting gangs and their organized crime networks as enemies, so blurring the boundaries between peacekeeping, peace enforcement and war making. By adopting a combative approach against gangs on behalf of the Haitian government, the MSS took an impartial stance toward the conflicting parties, conferring legitimacy on the state's response and closing off any possibility of engagement and dialogue with the gangs. But as the MSS was conceived as an atypical mission, it was authorized to use force without direct steering, backstopping and responsibility by the UN, which just engaged partially in the implementation of the mission's mandate by providing logistical and operational support (Le Cour/Oliveira/Herbert 2024: 30). Thus, the effectiveness and means used by the MSS in achieving its mandate were only associated with the discretion, capacity and resources by Kenya as a leading nation to manage the ad hoc coalition operation independently (cf. Tishkov 2025). Although the MSS received a clear call to limit the scope in the use of force in accordance to international human rights obligations, Resolution 2699 "appears to lack a clear definition of scope, since the leadership of the mission is to be given discretion over the resort to the use of force and the rules of engagement" (Le Cour/Oliveira/Herbert 2024: 33).

In practice, the MSS was confronted with a string of logistical, operative and tactical dilemmas that substantially undermined its capacity to factually achieve its mandate. Initially, the MSS faced a series of legal challenges to their deployment, due to the reluctance of the Kenyan parliament and the High Court to authorize troop dispatchment in Haiti (Tindi/Agwanda/Nyaburi 2024: 323) – and this redounded in a very late troop deployment (nine months after the passing of Resolution 2699), giving the gangs buffer time to reorganize themselves internally under a united front – through the formation of the *Viv Ansanm* alliance – and stockpile weapons to orchestrate solid resistance to MSS actions (Le Cour/Oliveira/Herbert 2024: 35). Notwithstanding the above, the most critical hurdles faced by the MSS related with its incapacity to secure enough troops, equipment and funding needed to fulfill the entirely of its mandate properly (ICG 2014: 12). Despite many initial troop pledges by more than twelve countries, the factual contingent contribution by third countries was meager than expected, with only five Central American and Caribbean countries actively taking part in the mission. From an envisioned 2,500-man force, the MSS only comprised less than 1,000 officers, representing approximately only 25% of the troop strength needed to symmetrically confront the gangs (Le Cour/Oliveira/Herbert 2024: 35). While Kenyan troops from different units of the Kenyan Police Service – such as the Rapid Deployment, General Service, Border Police and Anti-Stock Theft units – counted on extensive prior experience in dealing with insurgent groups in complex environments like in Democratic Republic of Congo, Somalia and South Sudan (Tishkov 2025: 371–372); overall, the MSS remained severely understaffed and faced considerable shortfalls in basic weapons and military equipment to conduct anti-gang raids in Port-au-Prince shantytowns, such as tactical vehicles, tanks, ballistic helmets, bullet-proof vests, ammunition, radios, night-vision goggles, drones and helicopters – without mention a deficit in intelligence (Mohor/Maçon/Kiage 2025, Reuters 2025). These shortcomings were also mirrored in the failure by the MSS to achieve other dimensions of the mandate granted to provide control of illicit trafficking of arms, ammunition and drugs at Haitian maritime and land crossing points due to the lack of border security infrastructure and coast guard vessel units (Le Cour/Oliveira/Herbert 2024: 36).

On par, the MSS faced severe financial and logistical constraints. As stated in Resolution 2699, the MSS was not funded directly by UN Department of Peace Operations budget, but implementing costs were borne by voluntary contributions of personnel, equipment, logistic resources and money for operating expenses from individual member states and regional organizations, managed through an UN trust fund (ICG 2024: 11). Since its launch, the MSS struggled with underfunding: although its initial annual cost was estimated at USD 600 million, it only achieved to raise around USD 115 million – largely with contributions from the United States and Canada – in the UN-managed trust fund (Tishkov 2025: 375). The disbursement of pledged funds was slow and jeopardized by a series of political positioning – such as the Trump administration's freeze on foreign aid spending to Haiti, which redounded negatively both in a delay in the mission's operational readiness, but also provoked disaffection and frustration among mission members due to non-payment of salaries and allowances (Blaise/Octave 2025, Waruru 2025). Along with this, MSS operational capacity was undermined by logistical constraints in the collaborative work with the PNH. In accordance with the mandate issued, MSS's task was to support the PNH in performing its law enforcement duties, but joint work and cooperation proved particularly challenging. On the one hand, the PNH is outmanned, outgunned, lacking facilities and budget, and ill-prepared to carry out complex anti-gang operations in a coordinated and effective manner alongside the MSS – which led to failures in command, planning and mutual tensions (Mohor/Maçon/ Kiage 2025, Exil 2025). On the other hand, as a byproduct of a long-standing process of institutional decay, the PNH is internally plagued by low morale, misconduct, and corruption among police officers – from rank-and-file officers to the upper echelons of the institution, some of whom were linked to criminal groups – and this sometimes resulted in the undermining of operational secrecy of mission planning and activities (ICG 2024: 16).

Despite these harsh limitations, the MSS was able to accomplish some modest advances in key gang strongholds, restoring order in certain gang-ridden areas of Port-au-Prince and regaining control of critical infrastructure – mainly police stations and correctional facilities – and transit locations, which temporarily pushed back the advance of gangs in the capital but displaced them to peripheral areas and the hinterland (Osoro 2025). In the few anti-gang raids undertaken, the mission operated under a cautious approach order to protect both civilians and its own personnel and avoid collateral damage, demonstrating a meaningful effort to avoid past mistakes in the misconduct of operations and causing negative unintended consequences (IPI 2024: 2). Indeed, in a wider sense, the MSS was given a broad mandate to tackle the side effects of peace operations, in areas such as preventing sexual exploitation and abuse, misconduct investigations, accountability mechanisms and appropriate wastewater management, but the mission lacked the real capacity to undertake all these tasks – largely due to the lack of personnel and resources to address these issues (ICG 2025: 17).

Perhaps the most critical issue in an examination of the MSS performance lies in its substantive contribution as a means of building social peace in Haiti. Despite "the operational design of the MSS mission was envisioned with four stages: deployment, decisive operations, stabilization and transition" (IPI 2024: 2), it failed to move beyond the first two dimensions, thus remaining unable to make a substantive contribution to improving the social and political situation in Haiti. This is largely attributed to the fact that the MSS was conceived as a sole temporary intervention force, without a clear plan to subsequently give way to a comprehensive UN peacekeeping mission (Le Cour/Oliveira/Herbert 2024: 30). Furthermore, because of its limited scope and capacities, the MSS was not really intended to end the gang problem once and for all, but just to allow the Haitian state to regain territorial control (ICG 2024: 15) – which in reality amounted to only temporary wins, as the mission failed to hold these areas permanently, arrest key gang leaders and large swaths of Port-au-Prince remained under gang control (ICG 2025: 17). For the MSS to realize its ambitious mandate, it needed greater resources, more time and a comprehensive strategy to structurally reform and reorganize the PNH and the justice system, addressing the underlying social and economic problems that caused gangs' expansion and consolidation (Tishkov 2025: 376), but also closer and stronger institutional cooperation with other UN agencies: Although the MSS operated in the field in parallel with the United Nations Integrated Office in Haiti (BINUH by its French acronym) – a special political mission tasked with the provision of advisory services and good offices for the Haitian government in areas like good governance, rule of law, political dialogue and human rights promotion – and more than twelve different UN agencies and programs, there was no real alignment and cooperation between these entities and the MSS, largely because the mission was not formally an UN-led operation and these other UN actors did not want to be directly implicated in the actions of the MSS (ICG 2024: 14).

Following the request of the Haitian government, suggestions by organized Haitian civil society and practitioners, and on recommendation of the UN Secretary General, on 30 September 2025 the UNSC – by a pen-drafted resolution from the US and Panama delegations – transitioned the MSS into the GSF by Resolution 2793: a mission five times the size of its predecessor, with a strengthened mandate and under a new format.

5 Assessment and Recommendations for the Gang Suppression Force

The experiences of MINUSTAH and the MSS yield a series of important lessons on the scope and limits of the use of coercive force by UN stabilization missions in Haiti, which in turn serve to map out a set of recommendations for the performance of the newly launched GSF and future engagement by the international community in the country.

As outlined in section 2, the use of coercive force by stabilization missions raises some critical issues on the rationale and futility of such actions by UN peace operations, which were clearly evidenced in the performance of MINUSTAH and the MSS. Both missions were launched under Chapter VII of the UN Charter to deal under a security and military-centric approach with an ongoing internal conflict and countering a designated peace aggressor that posed a threat to international peace and security; namely, they were authorized to use defensive and reactive coercive force to restore and uphold the Haitian state's authority and tackle criminal gangs in order to stabilize the security situation in the country. And under this resolve, both missions were given carte blanche to make use of all available means to achieve these ends – which in both cases involved conducting joint military-police gang-clearing operations – under unclear terms regarding the means allowed and boundaries. In doing so, both MINUSTAH and the MSS positioned themselves in a warring stance in favor of one of the conflicting parties –namely, the Haitian government – and thus relinquished the neutrality that constitutes one of the founding principles of UN peacekeeping.

Largely, both the ambiguity of the mandate and taking a partial position were unavoidable, both due to the political sensitivity of these mandates and the complex configuration and constellation of the UNSC, which undermine the use of clear and specific language on the nature and procedure of these actions, but whose ambiguity may prove positive in enabling a wide range of diverse options and strategies of varying scope to be implemented – as MINUSTAH did. Likewise, it is inevitable that missions under Chapter VII powers are biased toward the government and aimed at ensuring its protection and survival, because ultimately, for such peacekeeping operations to be legitimately licensed and deployed, they need the consent of the government in power. Moreover, from a moral standpoint, it is virtually impossible to remain entirely impartial to the contemptuous behavior committed by armed non-state actors of a criminal nature against the civilian population. Specifically in the Haitian case, these groups do not really vindicate the social, economic and political demands of the Haitian people, nor do they enjoy any social legitimacy for their actions – that is why the tension caused by the use of force with the principle of impartiality is a necessary evil that meets the fundamental objectives of the UN itself: to guarantee the integrity of states and observance of international peace and security, as well as to protect fundamental human rights in situations where human lives are at risk.

The conduct of counter-gang operations in Port-au-Prince *bidonvilles*, their achievements and side effects reflect the diametrically different experiences of MINUSTAH and the MSS. MINUSTAH engaged in a relatively successful manner in these raids because it enjoyed robust operational and tactical capabilities on-site, entailing the combination of a highly capable and well-equipped troop with access to a wide range of financial, material, technological and logistical resources – above all, highly valuable human and imagery intelligence useful for the planning and conduction of operations – that enabled MINUSTAH to factually dislocate and break up gangs. On the contrary, the MSS was a marginally trooped, equipped and funded mission that faced serious coordination and joint work challenges with its domestic counterpart (the PNH) and received poor logistical and operational support from the UN Secretariat, thus only achieving a few isolated and temporary gains. But as there are two sides to every coin, the actions of MINUSTAH and the MSS brought about a different record in terms of the negative unintended consequences of using force: While MINUSTAH incurred civilian casualties without any accountability or reparation for the victims, the MSS was much more cautious in conducting these raids in order to protect both civilians and its own personnel and avoid collateral damage.

Despite these strengths and shortcomings in each case, MINUSTAH and the MSS share a poor balance in terms of the ultimate futility of using coercive force as a means to long-term peacebuilding: Due to a strong focus on security, limited financial and material resources, the lack of a clear and larger plan for the reconstruction of Haiti and political will at the UNSC, poor cooperation with the (dysfunctional) Haitian institutions and joint work with UN agencies, the gains made after counter-gang operations deflated as the structural political, economic and social roots of the Haitian conflict remained unaddressed and unresolved.

The latest initiative by the international community to deal with the Haitian crisis is the GSF: a transition mission from the MSS, which does not merely constitute a name change, but is conceived as a complete reorganization of the mission's capabilities, personnel and its articulation with national forces and international actors (Fauriol/Speck 2025). The GSF was scaled up in numbers to 5,500 military and police officers and strengthened with additional capabilities and powers for conducting – independently or together with the PNH – gang-clearing operations and improving the overall security conditions of the country. The UNSC also granted the GSF a stronger, more offensive and more operational mandate to provide protection – in cooperation with the Haitian armed forces – for critical infrastructure sites and transit locations; control over land, maritime and air borders and ports; support the operational capacity building of the HNP and the army; and combat illicit trafficking of arms, ammunition, drugs and human beings (Mishra 2025). For accomplishing these tasks, the GSF is authorized – like its predecessors – to take all necessary measures to carry out its mandate and develop autonomously through the GSF Special Representative and the Force Commander its rules of engagement and any relevant directives on the use of force, whose deployment should ensure the highest standards of transparency, conduct and discipline for their contingents, and a robust compliance and oversight mechanisms to prevent, investigate and address misuse allegations.

The GSF is innovative in terms of its structure and relationship with the UN and other international actors present in the country. Like the MSS, the GSF is "a non-UN coalition under UN approval and oversight" (Ahmed 2025), namely, GSF operational command is held by a coalition of nations deployed under their own national flags – not as UN blue helmets – and it does not draw on the UN's assessed budget, but is funded through voluntary contributions located in a trust fund as the primary source of mission's resourcing (Valdmanis 2025). Political steering lies in the Standing Group of Partners (led by the United States and joined by the Bahamas, Canada, El Salvador, Guatemala, Jamaica and Kenya) to provide high-level strategic direction, oversight and relevant political decision-making for the GSF, while command and day-to-day operational decision-making remains under the Force Commander from Kenya – and both instances are requested to report regularly to the UNSC on the measures taken to mandate implementation. Under the novel GSF model, "peacekeeping is being somewhat outsourced – though under the UN legal and moral umbrella" (Ahmed 2025). For coordination and oversight, Resolution 2793 established a local-based UN Support Office in Haiti (UNSOH) as an umbrella liaison bureau to ensure coherent and unified action between all actors from the UN system, and provide swift and robust comprehensive logistical and operational support – including rations, housing, medical care, fuel, transportation, aviation, strategic communications and troop rotation – to the GSF, BINUH, the PNH and the mission of the Organization of American States (OAS) in Haiti (Mishra 2025, Valdmanis 2025). The launch of the GSF under this framework is symbolic of a shift in how collective security is organized, as UN steering now rests less on managing operations and commanding troops directly, but more on coordinating coalitions among its own agencies, member states, regional organizations and international NGOs (Ahmed 2025).

To a large extent – and not unfoundedly, a big question mark arises as to whether this newest undertaking by the UN in Haiti will do things differently than its predecessors, be able to cope effectively and sustainably with the criminal gangs, and finally steer the country toward a process of political, economic and social reconstruction endurable over time. To this end, it is recommended that the GSF performance should revive and put into practice a basic principle of counterinsurgency strategy as a pattern for action: "clear, hold and build" (cf. Karlsrud 2018), which allows for drawing up a set of actions for the long, medium and short term.

First, in the short term, GSF main priority task is to clear out the gangs through the use of high-intensity lethal force. Logically, doing so raises moral and legal debates regarding human rights and international law norms on the responsibility of perpetrators. But not doing so repeats fatal historical precedents of inaction by the UN to halt the commission of serious crimes against humanity, a process of profound social chaos and state deterioration. As shown in the previous experience under MINUSTAH, the use of force can be especially useful for removing or deterring those actors with whom no reconciliation or compromise could be found. And it seems that in the Haitian case, there is no real alternative but to kill key gang leaders, because their crimes and demands for negotiation are largely unacceptable. Overall, the legitimacy of initiating a political negotiation process with the gangs has raised serious questions both within Haitian society and abroad, because the gangs have conditioned negotiations only after the granting of broad safeguards that include comprehensive immunity from criminal prosecution, the possibility of competing in elections, and even the issuance of passports for all gang members and the opportunity to seek political asylum abroad – and these demands are unacceptable to both politicians and the majority of the population.

To effectively conduct gang-clearing operations, GSF activities will require the provision of greater material and technological resources to employ high-intensity lethal force more efficiently, since Haitian gangs today are more militarily powerful, networked and resilient than those during the MINUSTAH intervention. Consequently, to fulfill its mandate successfully, the GSF must have at its disposal the resources and capabilities necessary to mount, articulate and sustain well-equipped forces in the field, including the supply of specialized military and police units, aviation support, robust all-terrain vehicles, high-technology weapons and ammunition, as well as reconnaissance and surveillance assets. Above all, it requires three key tools for success: a well-trained force to carry out operations in gang-controlled areas, ideally with expertise in dealing with urban policing challenges in hostile environments; the incorporation of human and aerial intelligence to gather key data for the preparation of operations; and the execution of these operations under thorough preparation and with clear rules of engagement on the use of force, establishing mechanisms to prevent collateral harm to civilians and the negative consequences of the use of force during such raids. And to put these measures into practice, the GSF is granted by Resolution 2793 operational autonomy to act independently and not have its hands tied when faced with hurdles for joint work with the PNH.

Through a clearance strategy, the GSF should not become a blanket death squad, especially considering that a significant proportion of gang members are minors, as a result of systematic forced recruitment. As part of clearing operations, the GSF should also devote efforts to isolate and deter gangs by non-lethal means. To this end, the mission was given temporary and exceptional powers to conduct arrests and detentions, and these procedures should apply to mid- and low-range gang members – and, in particular, ensure that children apprehended in such operations are referred to child protection actors and confined to adult prisons. And in order to ensure that these confinements yield a long-term multiplier effect, they should be ideally coupled with rehabilitation and reintegration programs, psychosocial support and access to education or vocational training.

So far, the GSF seems to be conceived essentially as a rapid reaction force with an initial one-year mandate; therefore, during this time, it should focus as much force, resources and capacity as possible on neutralizing and breaking the gangs through coercive force – which is not a bad thing per se, as long as this mission serves as the first pillar of a recovery plan and a precursor to a full-fledged UN peacekeeping mission. In other cases worldwide, the international community has used force with some success at the operational and tactical levels to coerce, suppress and destroy sources of instability, but it has not shown an ability to harness the futility of force towards statebuilding and consolidation. Therefore, force alone has proven incapable of solving in the long term the structural problems of a political and social nature that cause the genesis and actuation of armed non-state actors of a criminal nature. Therefore, after clearing the gangs in the short term, it is imperative to adopt a series of follow-up actions in the medium and long term aimed at holding wins and structurally rebuilding the Haitian state. To design and implement these measures, the GSF should draw on past successes but also be forward-thinking and follow valuable recommendations from scholars and practitioners on how to improve UN peacekeeping, which suggest a mix of adaptation through lesson learning and innovation.

To this end, secondly, the GSF must hold the recovered territories and the defeat of the gangs in the medium term. Three tasks are prioritized for this purpose: the implementation of a comprehensive program of disarmament, demobilization and reintegration for former gang members at the local level, tailored with training and employment initiatives for young people, who make up the base of the gang pyramid but joined them as a result of a lack of prospects and unemployment. For this reason, it is worth reviving past successful initiatives such as locally based socio-economic assistance programs, including quick-impact projects for community violence prevention. Nor should it be overlooked that gangs have long been a constituent part of Haiti's bottom-up security governance architecture, largely due to the absence of a functional central state and delegitimized state security forces. Consequently, it would be worth considering whether, as part of demobilization and reintegration processes for former gang members, community policing programs could be put in place aimed at decentralizing public order production through existing grassroots community organizations (or *baz*) engaged in local governance. And following UN recommendations, it is essential to implement gender-centered approaches to address the effects of gang-related gender-based violence, "involving women and girls in the identification of solutions and building the capacity of institutions in which women can trust and create cross-sectoral collaboration to provide services that are tailored for women and girls" (Le Cour/Oliveira/Herbert 2024: 31). Hence, within the framework of neighborhood organizations, it would also be worthwhile to draw on the positive experience of the all-female formed police units deployed by Bangladesh under MINUSTAH from 2010 to 2017, which promoted the inclusion of local women – in many cases victims of sexual violence – in preventive community policing programs as a means of psychological rehabilitation and social reintegration (cf. Gandbhir/Obaid-Chinoy 2015, Huddleston 2022).

The second task to be accomplished in the medium term involves the implementation of a capacity-building program for the police and justice system. It is essential that post-clearing containment builds up Haiti's own capacity to maintain security rather than sustaining a long-term foreign occupation force. To this end, it is imperative to bolster the institutional strength of the PNH and the Haitian army through a resource allocation package, security sector reform programs, and capacity building strategies. The EU and the OAS already committed in early November 2025 to develop a partnership initiative to support these endeavors (Sénat 2025). Internally, the PNH urgently needs a crusade to root out the corruption prevailing within the institution, as the connections between gangs and police must be dismantled through a robust anti-corruption plan: "Officers with ties to gangs or criminal networks must be vetted and removed, while recruitment processes must be made transparent and insulated from outside influence. To achieve this, Haiti needs a strong, well-protected system capable of maintaining the integrity of the vetting process. International partners will be key in the early stages, helping to ensure that criminal actors cannot undermine or corrupt the plan" (Randolph 2025). To achieve this goal, the positive example of Kosovo could be emulated, where a rule of law mission could be established for joint management of the justice system between Haitians and international lawyers and implementing justice sector reform, fighting against corruption and even supporting the independence and accountability of rule of law institutions.

A third key task for holding the gangs involves adopting measures to dismantle the political economy surrounding their raison d'être, or in other words, breaking the hidden criminal links between gangs, politicians, businesspeople and organized crime networks. Domestically, it is worthwhile to continue applying vetoes to high-ranking politicians tied to illegal activities with gangs – as has been done so far through economic sanctions and removal from office of TPC members. Internationally, transnational organized crime networks of drug and arms trafficking operating in the Caribbean, which constitute the new gang principals, should also be dismantled – perhaps the Trump Administration's current military movements in the Caribbean Basin are a first step in this direction.

In fact, the ultimate futility of using coercive force by peace operations to manage conflicts and deal with peace spoilers depends not only on how effectively this is done from an operational and technical sense but, more crucially, on whether these actions are aligned with a broader political project to advance in building sustainable societal peace and addressing the structural causes of conflict. What matters is that the use of force by peace operations does not become an end itself, but it must serve long-term political and strategic objectives, particularly supporting a broader political agenda by creating a secure environment where constructive political processes may take place and the underlying socio-economic causes and drivers of conflict and violence be properly addressed – and so translating the operational and tactical outcomes of using coercive force into sustainable political gains. Consequently, the GSF should serve as a springboard for the launching and implementation of a comprehensive plan entailing a strategy including political and governance reform, as well as long-term socio-economic development. Therefore, thirdly, after clear and hold, UN engagement in Haiti should devote efforts to build in the long term, ideally through a sustained and multidimensional presence of at least 10 to 15 years.

Founding Haiti anew calls for a holistic package of political reform and economic recovery, in close collaboration among Haitian institutions and international agencies without undermining national sovereignty and self-determination of the Haitian people. On the one hand, since establishing a UN interim administration is hardly viable and feasible and would have little domestic legitimacy – due to previous bad experiences of imperialism and international tutelage in Haitian history, the international community should support (mainly through UNSOH and BINUH) the realization of the measures outlined in the basic agreement achieved among Haitian political actors as the foundation of the TPC, which call for a legal-normative process of constitutional reform to reshape the country's political system and the holding of general elections to renew all public powers. On the other hand, while it is true that the Haitian government bears primary responsibility for the well-being of its population, it cannot be denied that the Haitian state suffers from chronic dysfunction, lacks institutional capacity and is virtually bankrupt. For this reason, the country is in need of active and high-intensity assistance from the international community to initiate, fund and implement a plan for humanitarian aid delivery and economic development. This daunting task requires better coordination, financing and strengthening of existing efforts by various UN humanitarian and development agencies already work-ing in Haiti, as well as engaging regional organizations such as the OAS and Caricom in these endeavors through peacekeeping partnerships, in a way for decentralizing efforts and enhancing responsiveness and regional ownership in the management and resolution of the Haitian question (Ahmed 2025).

In sum and as a closing remark, UN peace operations in Haiti may be in a position to use coercive force to counter obstructionist violence and defeat spoilers, but for this to result in long-term political capital, it is imperative to interlink coercive force with a broader strategy that embraces a reform of the political system, comprehensive economic recovery, security sector reform, development and humanitarian aid, reconciliation and transitional justice processes, and confidence-building measures. While it is true that all these efforts are ambitious and demand a significant investment of time, thorough planning and money – which is not easily and swiftly available under such complex multilateral settings, the longest journey is the one that is never started. So, it is critical to take the first steps in this direction decisively and at a solid, consistent and sustained pace. To achieve these ends, not only should the international community finally commit itself wholeheartedly to a reconstruction plan, but the Haitian people must also cooperate and do their best to overcome the past and build a better future for themselves, their country and future generations. The success of the ongoing UN undertaking in Haiti is not only key to refounding the country anew, vindicating the reputation of UN peacekeeping and the futility of using coercive force by peace operations, but it could provide a practical blueprint for the launching of future efforts in other similar contexts where a state is gradually falling apart and its population is being brutalized by the horrific crimes perpetrated by ruthless and criminal armed non-state actors, where the UN has been unfruitful involved for a long time, and an unprecedented humanitarian crisis is currently unfolding before the world's helpless eyes – such as Sudan.

References

Ahmed, Bulbul (2025): The UN is reinventing peacekeeping – Haiti is the testing ground. *The Conversation*, 11 November. Available online at https://theconversa tion.com/the-un-is-reinventing-peacekeeping-haiti-is-the-testing-ground-268267, checked on 30 November 2025.

Aoi, Chiyuki/De Coning, Cedric/Thakur, Ramesh (2010): *Unintended Consequences of Peacekeeping Operations*. Tokyo/New York: United Nations University Press.

Berdal, Mats (2019): What Are the Limits to the Use of Force in UN Peacekeeping? In Cedric De Coning/Mateja Peter (eds.): *United Nations Peace Operations in a Changing Global Order*. Cham: Palgrave Macmillan, pp. 113–131.

Berdal, Mats/Ucko, David (2015): The Use of Force in UN Peacekeeping Operations. Problems and Prospects. In *The Rusi Journal* 160 (1), pp. 6–12.

Blaise, Juhakenson (2025a): Haiti leaders abandon costly effort to replace 1987 Constitution. *Haitian Times*, 13 October. Available online at haitiantimes.com/2025/10/13/haiti-constitutional-referendum/, checked on 14 November 2025.

Blaise, Juhakenson (2025b): Haiti elections 'impossible' by 2026 government turnover deadline. *Haitian Times*, 11 April. Available online at https://haitian times.com/2025/11/04/haiti-elections-impossible-for-2026-turnover/, checked on 14 November 2025.

Blaise, Juhakenson (2025c): For 36th year, US renews Haiti's designation as major drug transit route. *Haitian Times*, 26 September. Available online at https://haitiantimes.com/2025/09/26/haiti-trump-drug-transit-designation/, checked on 3 November 2025.

Blaise, Juhakenson/Octave, Fritznel (2025): Did US funding for Haiti's security mission stop? The Haitian Times breaks it down. *Haitian Times*, 28 February. Available online at https://haitiantimes.com/2025/02/28/us-aid-haiti-security-mission/, checked on 29 November 2025.

Cockayne, James (2014): The Futility of Force? Strategic Lessons for Dealing with Unconventional Armed Groups from the UN's War on Haiti's Gangs. In *Journal of Strategic Studies* 37 (5), pp. 736–769.

De Coning, Cedric (2018): Is stabilization the new normal? Implications of stabilization mandates for the use of force in UN peacekeeping operations. In Peter Nadin (ed.): *The Use of Force in UN Peacekeeping*. London/New York: Routledge, pp. 85–99.

Di Razza, Namie (2020): *The Accountability System for the Protection of Civilians in UN Peacekeeping*. IPI Reports. New York: International Peace Institute.

Dorn, Walter (2009): Intelligence-led Peacekeeping: The United Nations Stabilization Mission in Haiti (MINUSTAH), 2006–07. In *Intelligence and National Security* 24 (6), pp. 805–835.

Dorn, Walter (2018): Protecting civilians with force: Dilemmas and lessons from the UN stabilization mission in Haiti. In Peter Nadin (ed.): *The Use of Force in UN Peacekeeping*. London/New York: Routledge, pp. 124–144.

Ekanayake, Charuka (2021): *Regulating the Use of Force by United Nations Peace Support Operations. Balancing Promises and Outcomes*. London/New York: Routledge.

Exil, Sandrine (2025): Kenyan soldiers in Haiti frustrated over mission burden: "all the risk falls on us". *EFE*, 14 May. Available online at https://efe.com/en/other-news/2025-05-14/kenyan-soldiers-haiti-frustrated-mission/, checked on 28 November 2025.

Fauriol, Georges/Speck, Mary (2025): The United States Votes to Establish a Haiti Gang Suppression Force: Now What?. *Center for Strategic & International Studies*, 8 October May. Available online at https://www.csis.org/analysis/united-states-votes-establish-haiti-gang-suppression-force-now-what/, checked on 28 November 2025.

Foley, Conor (2017): *UN Peacekeeping Operations and the Protection of Civilians*. New York: Cambridge University Press.

Fragile States Index (2024): *Country Dashboard: Haiti*. Available online at https://fragilestatesindex.org/country-data/haiti, checked on 28 September 2025.

Francisque, Edxon (2025): Haiti-Investigation: Child disappearance near border reignites fears of organ trafficking in Haiti amid stalled investigation. *Haitian Times*, 24 June. Available online at https://haitiantimes.com/2025/07/24/haitian-child-disappearance-abduction-and-rumors-of-organ-trafficking/, checked on 13 November 2025.

Friesendorf, Cornelius (2012): *International Intervention and the Use of Force: Military and Police Roles*. SSR Paper 4. Geneva: Geneva Centre for the Democratic Control of Armed Forces.

Gandbhir, Geeta/Obaid-Chinoy, Sharmeen (2015): *A Journey of a Thousand Miles: Peacekeepers*. G2P2 Films. USA/Bangladesh, 95 min.

Girard, Philippe (2010): *Haiti. The Tumultuous History – From Pearl of the Caribbean to Broken Nation*. 2nd ed. New York: Palgrave Macmillan.

Harvard College (2021): *Killing with Impunity: State-Sanctioned Massacres in Haiti*. Cambridge: Harvard College.

Huddleston, Evening (2022): *Advancing United Nation's Gender Mainstreaming: Female Peacekeepers in Haiti and Liberia*. Unpublished bachelor's thesis. New York, Fordham University.

Hunt, Charles (2017): All necessary means to what ends? The unintended consequences of the 'robust turn' in UN peace operations. In *International Peacekeeping* 24 (1), pp. 108–131.

Hunt, Charles (2019): Analyzing the Co-Evolution of the Responsibility to Protect and the Protection of Civilians in UN Peace Operations. In *International Peacekeeping* 26 (5), pp. 630–659.

International Crisis Group (2024): *Haiti Gangs: Can a Foreign Mission Break Their Stranglehold?*. Latin America and Caribbean Briefing N° 49. Port-au-Prince/Brussels: International Crisis Group.

International Crisis Group (2025): *Locked in Transition: Politics and Violence in Haiti*. Latin American and Caribbean Report N° 107. Port-au-Prince/Brussels: International Crisis Group.

International Peace Institute (2024): *Emerging Practices in New Mission Models: The Multinational Security Support Mission in Haiti*. New York: International Peace Institute.

Karlsrud, John (2018): *The UN at War*. Cham: Springer.

Karlsrud, John (2019): From Liberal Peacebuilding to Stabilization and Counter-terrorism. In *International Peacekeeping* 26 (1), pp. 1–21.

Kenkel, Kai (2013): Five generations of peace operations: From the "thin blue line" to "painting a country blue". In *Revista Brasileira de Política Internacional* 56 (1), pp. 122–143.

Kolbe, Athena (2013): *Revisiting Haiti's Gangs and Organized Violence*. HASOW Discussion Paper 5. Rio de Janeiro: HASOW.

Le Cour, Romain/Oliveira, Ana/Herbert, Matt (2024): *A Critical Moment. Haiti's gang crisis and international responses*. Geneva: Global Initiative Against Transnational Organized Crime.

Lemay-Hébert, Nicolas (2017): United Nations Stabilization Mission in Haiti (MINUSTAH). In Joachim Koops et al (eds.): *The Oxford handbook of United Nations peacekeeping operations*. Oxford/New York: Oxford University Press, pp. 720–730.

Lundahl, Mats (2012): *The political economy of disaster and underdevelopment. Destitution, plunder and earthquake in Haiti*. New York: Routledge.

Mishra, Vibhu (2025): UN Security Council approves new 'suppression force' for Haiti amid spiraling gang violence. *UN News*, 30 September. Available online at https://news.un.org/en/story/2025/09/1166006, checked on 20 November 2025.

Mistler-Ferguson, Scott (2022): G9 vs. G-PEP – The Two Gang Alliances Tearing Haiti Apart. *Insight Crime*, 21 July. Available online at https://insightcrime.org/news/g9-gpep-two-gang-alliances-tearing-haiti-apart/, checked on 9/15/2025.

Mohor, Daniela/Maçon, Dumas/Kiage, Nyaboga (2025): Haiti in-depth: Why the Kenya-led security mission is floundering. *The New Humanitarian*, 13 January. Available online at https://www.thenewhumanitarian.org/investigations/2025/01/13/haiti-depth-why-kenya-led-security-mission-floundering, checked on 26 November 2025.

Office of the High Commissioner for Human Rights (2025): High Commissioner Türk updates Human Rights Council on Haiti: We can – and must – turn this situation around. *OHCHR*, 10 February. Available online at https://www.ohchr.org/en/statements-and-speeches/2025/10/high-commissioner-turk-updates-human-rights-council-haiti-we-can, checked on 14 November 2025.

Osoro, Timothy (2025): Kenyan Police in Haiti Celebrate Major Wins So Far as Mission Enters Operations Stage. *The Kenyan Times*, 6 August. Available online at https://thekenyatimes.com/latest-kenya-times-news/kenyan-police-in-haiti-celebrate-major-wins-so-far-as-mission-enters-operations-stage/, checked on 29 November 2025.

Pingeot, Lou (2018): United Nations peace operations as international practices: Revisiting the UN mission's armed raids against gangs in Haiti. In *European Journal of International Security* 3 (3), pp. 364–381.

Randolph, Kirk (2025): Haiti's Security Crisis: The Multinational Mission's Role and What Comes Next. *United States Institute of Peace*, 16 January. Available online at https://www.usip.org/publications/2025/01/haitis-security-crisis-multinational-missions-role-and-what-comes-next, checked on 29 November 2025.

Reuters (2025): A year in, Haiti mission leader warns of shortfalls in troops, funds, gear. *Reuters*, 16 June. Available online at https://www.reuters.com/world/

americas/year-haiti-mission-leader-warns-shortfalls-troops-funds-gear-2025-06-26/?utm, checked on 28 November 2025.

Schuberth, Moritz (2015): A transformation from political to criminal violence? Politics, organised crime and the shifting functions of Haiti's urban armed groups. In *Conflict, Security & Development* 15 (2), pp. 169–196.

Sénat, Jean (2025): OAS and EU Pledge Support to Bolster Haiti's Police and Anti-Gang Force. *Le Nouvelliste*, 4 November. Available online at https://lenouvelliste.com/en/article/261402/oas-and-eu-pledge-support-to-bolster-haitis-police-and-anti-gang-force, checked on 30 November 2025.

Thakur, Ramesh (2018): *Reviewing the Responsibility to Protect. Origins, Implementation and Controversies*. Milton: Routledge.

The Independent (2017): UN peacekeepers in Haiti implicated in child sex ring. *The Independent*, 14 April. Available online at https://www.independent.co.uk/news/world/americas/un-haiti-peacekeepers-child-sex-ring-sri-lankan-underage-girls-boys-teenage-a7681966.html, checked on 25 November 2025.

Tindi, James/Agwanda, Billy/Nyadera, Israel (2024): The Dilemma of Troop Contribution to International Peace Missions: a Case of the Kenya Police Deployment to Haiti. In *Journal of International Peacekeeping* 27 (3), pp. 320–341.

Tishkov, Sergey (2025): Leadership of the Republic of Kenya in the Multinational Security Support Mission for Haiti: Experience and lessons for ad hoc coalitions. In *Vestnik RUDN. International Relations* 25 (3), pp. 366–381.

United Nations Development Programme (2023): *Human Development Insights 2023*. Available online at https://hdr.undp.org/data-center/country-insights#/ranks, checked on 30 September 2025.

United Nations Integrated Office in Haiti (2025a): *Intensification of Criminal Violence in Lower Artibonite, the Centre Department, and Regions Located East of the Metropolitan Area of Port-Au-Prince*. Port-au-Prince: United Nations Human Rights, Office of the High Commissioner.

United Nations Integrated Office in Haiti (2025b): *Report of the Secretary-General*. New York: UNSC.

United Nations Integrated Office in Haiti (2025c): *Quarterly Report on the Human Rights Situation in Haiti. July–September 2025*. Port-au-Prince: BINUH.

United Nations Office on Drugs and Crime (UNODC) (7/2/2025): *UN Security Council Briefing on the Situation in Haiti*. Vienna: UNODC. Available online at https://www.unodc.org/unodc/en/speeches/2025/020725-unsc-briefing-haiti.html, checked on 21 November 2025.

United Nations Security Council (UNSC) (2004): Resolution 1542, 30 April.

United Nations Security Council (UNSC) (2005): Resolution 1608, 22 June.

United Nations Security Council (UNSC) (2023): Resolution 2699, 2 October.

United Nations Security Council (UNSC) (2025): Resolution 2793, 30 September.

Valdmanis, Vincent (2025): Turning the Tide in Haiti: The Gang Suppression Force Explained. *Better World Campaign*, 10 January. Available online at https://betterworldcampaign.org/expert-analysis/turning-the-tide-in-haiti-the-gang-suppression-force-explained, checked on 21 November 2025.

Wakefield, Jacqui/Giles, Christopher/Cheetham, Joshua (2025): Smugglers' paradise: How US guns flow to gang-ravaged Haiti. *BBC*, 17 April. Available online at https://www.bbc.com/news/articles/cly15pp707go, checked on 15 November 2025.

Waruru, Maina (2025): In Haiti, Kenyan police officers between anger and power-lessness. *Afrique XXI*, 6 January. Available online at https://afriquexxi.info/In-Haiti-Kenyan-police-officers-between-anger-and-powerlessness, checked on 27 November 2025.

Williams, Paul/Bellamy, Alex (2021): *Understanding Peacekeeping*. 3rd ed. Cambridge: Polity.

Wills, Siobhán/McLaughin, Cahal (2017): *It Stays With You – Use of Force by Peacekeepers in Haiti*. Queen's University Belfast, Film Studies Department. Bois Neuf/Cité Soleil/Belfast, 51:49 min. Available online at https://itstays withyou.com/full-film/.

World Bank (2025): *Haiti: Overview*. Available online at https://www.worldbank.org/en/country/haiti/overview, checked on 28 September 2025.

Subject Index

The Author

Stiven Tremaria studied History and International Relations at the Central University of Venezuela and holds a Ph.D. in Political Sciences from the University of Osnabrück. He is currently a research associate at the Department of International Police Relations at the German Police University and acting executive secretary of the Academic Forum for International Security (WIFIS e.V). His main fields of interest are international security policy, police and military research, autocratization studies and comparative politics. He has extensive academic and professional experience abroad gathered through exchanges, work and field research – including in Haiti, where he served between 2010 and 2011 as a liaison officer to the Interim Haiti Recovery Commission seated in Port-au-Prince.

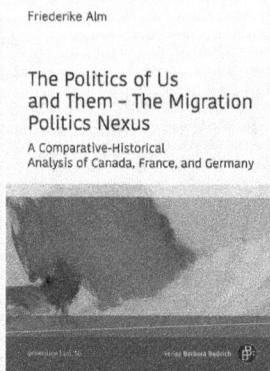

Friederike Alm

The Politics of Us
and Them – The Migration
Politics Nexus
A Comparative-Historical
Analysis of Canada, France, and Germany

The Politics of Us and Them – The Migration Politics Nexus

A Comparative-Historical Analysis
of Canada, France, and Germany

promotion, volume 16
2025 • approx. 400 pp. • Pb. • approx. 89,90 € (D) • 92,50 € (A)
ISBN 978-3-8474-3136-7 • eISBN 978-3-8474-3271-5
available as e-book in open access

Canada, France, and Germany share many similarities, for example, their democratic principles and constitutional commitment to human rights and equal opportunities. However, each country approaches immigration differently.

Friederike Alm presents a comparative-historical analysis which sheds light on the historical trajectory of migration politics in the three countries since 1945. The author proposes a new concept for migration research, the migration politics nexus, which highlights the interconnection between immigration, citizenship, and integration politics.

shop.budrich.de

GPSR Authorized Representative: Easy Access System Europe, Mustamäe tee 50, 10621 Tallinn, Estonia, gpsr.requests@easproject.com